Learn'Em
Good
-Writing-

Improve Your Child's <u>Writing</u> Skills:
Simple and Effective Ways to
Become Your Child's Writing Tutor at
Home

Stuart Ackerman MSc.Ed, B.A.
www.tutorgiant.com

This book is dedicated to my mother, who made sure I had strong language skills as a child.

Watch for the following Learn'Em Good books:

Learn'Em Good Writing
Learn'Em Good Reading
Learn'Em Good ADD/ADHD
Learn'Em Good Grammar
Learn'Em Good Homeschooling
Learn'Em Good Learning Disabilities
Learn'Em Good Social Skills
Learn'Em Good Homework and Studying

Use the following code to receive 50% off any Tutorgiant.com membership with the purchase of this book.

4FM8T

CHAPTER TITLE

Learn'Em Good

CHAPTER TITLE

Acknowledgements

I would like to thank my sons for inspiring me to achieve.

Table of Contents
(not continents)
Part 1

Ways to Learn'Em Good at Home

Table of Contents
Part 2
Ways to Learn'Em Good at Home

Table of Contents
Part 3
Bonus Lessons from Tutorgiant.com

Introduction

The ability to write is one of the most important skills you can impart to your child. Regardless of the future vocation your child chooses, he or she will require highly developed writing skills.

The ability to write is like riding a bike. That is, once your child can do it, it is his or hers forever.

There are several reasons why you should help your child to write at home:

1. Your child's grades in school will improve.
2. Your child will improve his or her self expression.
3. Your child will have a better chance getting a college or university degree.
4. Writing skills have a direct correlation to your child's future job success and socio-economic status.
5. Your family will spend quality time together.
6. Your child will have greater confidence in his or her writing and overall scholastic abilities.

When I refer to 'writing', I'm not restricting it to just a pencil and paper. Using a word processor or other technological tool require the same basic writing principles as to writing manually. What I am referring to, is the ability to convey thoughts onto a physical surface, construct sentences, paragraphs, ideas, and the mechanics of writing itself. Writing is more than putting words on paper. It is the final stage of 'thinking'.

Parents don't realize that they can have a major impact on their child's writing skills. I realize, as a teacher, that most parents are not familiar with the curriculum in their state or province (that's why I wrote this book). It is difficult for most parents to know how to properly format a paragraph, organize a report, or write an explanation. These types of writing are taught and assessed in the classroom. What parents can help their children with though, are the 'practical' writing skills that should be practiced at home.

The first section in this book gives you 26 ways to help your child write at home. Every idea shows you how to incorporate the specific piece of writing, what to look for, and how it will help your child according to the curriculum (i.e. skills that are taught and assessed in school). All 'what to look for's' will be explained in more detail in the second section. Try to use the ideas found in the first section according to your child's age level and abilities. For example, let's assume you want your child to write a 'thank you' card for a birthday present. You should have fewer expectations from a grade 1 child as opposed to a grade 6 student. I will outline these expectations under each writing idea.

The second section gives you practical ways to help your child improve his or her writing in specific areas such as: using quotation marks, writing a report, constructing a paragraph, etc…
Use can use this section to help your child when he or she comes home with a specific writing task (e.g. a personal narrative essay) and requires help.

This book is suited for parents with children in grades 1-6 and even grades 7-8 who require some extra reinforcement of their writing skills at home.

Good luck and Learn'Em Good!

Stuart Ackerman

Part 1
Learn'Em Good
Idea #1

Create a Family Dinner Menu

Let your child create and write the menu for a family dinner while you do the cooking. Help your child spell out the difficult words or get your child to use a dictionary. You can have your child write a menu for one meal or for an entire week of meals. Your child can even help you with the grocery shopping! Make sure you show your child the format of a menu in advance (e.g. a delivery menu that you have in a drawer).

What to Look For

For younger kids, look for proper spelling and capital letters. Older students should add in adjectives (descriptive words) to make the food 'sound' more appetizing (e.g. succulent). Make sure your child organizes the food into sections (e.g. appetizer, entrée, dessert).

Connections to the Curriculum

- spelling
- organization
- media literacy (creating a menu)
- word choice (i.e. using descriptive words)
- grammar (adjectives)

Learn'Em Good
Idea #2

A Picture Says a Thousand Words – Now Write Them

After your have taken some pictures from your family vacation, special outing (e.g. the zoo, a park), or special event (e.g. school play, baseball finals), create a journal/scrapbook with your child. Have your child put the pictures in chronological order. Then, get your child to write a caption (i.e. a sentence for younger kids to a paragraph for older ones) about the event. Your child can include the details of the picture (i.e. who, when, where etc…), his or her feelings at the time, and why that picture is special.

What to Look For

For younger kids, look for proper spelling, capitals and periods. Older students should use good adjectives and adverbs to express their 'voice'. Their writing should have a 'mood' (hopefully a happy one).

Connections to the Curriculum

- spelling
- chronological order
- the writing skill of 'voice'
- word choice (i.e. using descriptive words)
- grammar (adjectives, adverbs)
- descriptive sentences

Learn'Em Good
Idea #3

Picture Stories

You can cut out a picture from a magazine or print one off the internet. Younger children can draw their own picture. Have your child write a story about the picture. You can get your child to choose the picture or make it apply to your child's current unit of study in school. For example, your grade 3 might be learning about plants and soil. You can try to get a picture of the demolition of the rainforests, or a child picking a flower from a garden. Your grade 5 child, who is studying ancient civilizations, can use a picture of the Great Pyramids of Giza to write a story. The possibilities are endless.

What to Look For

For younger kids, look for the proper use of tenses (i.e. the entire story should be told in the same tense), spelling, and a beginning, middle, and end. Older students should focus on the main characters, a chronological plot or story line, and different settings. Older students should also include facts that they learn in class about that specific subject area if you are making the story fit in with science or social studies. All students can also work on the proper use of quotation marks.

Connections to the Curriculum

- spelling, specific vocabulary
- character, plot, setting
- punctuation (quotation marks)
- verb tenses

Learn'Em Good
Idea #4

Saying 'Thank You' to a Professional

We always teach our children to say 'thank you', but we rarely have them write it. The next time your child goes to the dentist, doctor, veterinarian, or any other professional who helps, have your child write a thank you card. This can be written with a paper and pencil or typed on the computer. Ask your child what he or she plans on saying before writing it in the card.

What to Look For

Students at every level should focus on properly addressing the individual (i.e. Dear…,), a paragraph (also called the body), and a closing (e.g. Yours Truly…). Make sure your child 'specifically' writes down that which he or she is thankful for.

Connections to the Curriculum

- specific writing format of a letter
- voice
- understanding the reason for writing
- punctuation (commas)
- clarity and coherence
- developing ideas

Learn'Em Good
Idea #5

Setting Goals

It is important for students, especially those who need to improve their writing grades, to set goals for the next term. You can get your child to write down some goals that he or she plans on attaining in school and how he or she will achieve them. Your child can write down the goal, and under it, the ways he or she plans on achieving them. This is similar to a procedure. That is, your child will write down the goal, 'I will get better grades in writing next term'. Under this goal, your child can list his or her plan (e.g. "1. I will…", "2. I plan on…").

What to Look For

All students work on procedure writing in class. Look for a clear introduction as to what the procedure is about (it should state this in the first sentence), and make sure the list is in some sort of chronological or logical order. Instead of listing the plan numerically, your child can use transition words to 'link' his or her ideas.

Connections to the Curriculum

- procedure writing
- list writing
- organization
- time order sequence
- linking/transition words

Learn'Em Good
Idea #6

Thanksgiving Writing

Students of all ages will enjoy this one. Before Thanksgiving, have your child write down what he or she is thankful for. Your child should have this written out before Thanksgiving dinner. Then, have your child read it out loud to the family before you eat. This will help your child improve both writing and oral communication skills.

What to Look For

You can choose what you want to work on with younger kids (e.g. sentence structure, voice, organization). Since your child will be reading out loud, make sure your child focuses on sentence fluency (i.e. how the sentences sound). Older students should focus on 'supporting details'. That is, they should not only write what they are grateful for, but they should also write 'why' they are grateful for those things.

Connections to the Curriculum

- spelling, punctuation
- supporting details
- procedure/list writing
- writing for an intended audience
- sentence fluency
- descriptive paragraphs
- developing ideas

19

Learn'Em Good
Idea #7

Create a Phone Book

Younger students can practice both number and writing skills with this one. Have your child write down the names, addresses, and phone numbers of friends and/or relatives who your child often calls. Older children can do the same but they could add in a descriptive caption under the person's name (e.g. My fantastic uncle who…).

What to Look For

Focus on organization, capital letters, and the proper spelling of numbers (e.g. forty-two) with younger students. Older students can also work on organization as well; they can work on descriptive words (i.e. word choice).

Connections to the Curriculum

- spelling
- capital letters
- organization
- descriptive words (word choice)
- number literacy

Learn'Em Good
Idea #8

Happy Birthday!

Let your child write out the invitations for his or her birthday. This is a great way for your child to see that practical applications for writing. You can have your child follow the prompts in a store bought invitation, or your child can create his or her own on the computer. Older students can use the computer to print out an invitation and they can write a few lines to a paragraph explaining how much fun the party will be.

What to Look For

For younger students, focus on following directions and using capital letters. Your younger child should also pay attention to the writing prompts (e.g. time, location, etc...). Older students should focus on descriptive writing (i.e. using descriptive verbs to describe the fun other kids will have) and proper grammar.

Connections to the Curriculum

- spelling,
- capital letters
- following directions
- descriptive writing (verbs, adverbs)
- writing for an intended audience
- media literacy (using a word processor for writing)

Learn'Em Good
Idea #9

A is for Alliteration

Younger students can go on a scavenger hunt at home to find objects around the house that begin with each letter. They can also look in books for animals or find any other list. Have your child write an alphabetical alliteration poem. For example, "All the alligators ate apples, Busy bees buzz by…" Older students (I've had grade 5's really enjoy this activity) can do the same activity, especially if they create a power point presentation.

What to Look For

For all students, look for 'word choice' skills. Word choice refers to choosing uncommon words. Your child can use a dictionary and a thesaurus. Younger students can focus on rhyming while older ones can focus on using a dictionary and thesaurus.

Connections to the Curriculum

- word choice
- grammar (adjectives, verbs, adverbs)
- organizing ideas

Learn'Em Good
Idea #10

Share Your Writing from Work

A great way to model writing, and, to get your child interested in writing is to show him the writing you do at work. Bring home some samples (good ones of course) of the writing you do at work. This will show your child that he or she is not the only one writing at home. It will also help your child realize that writing doesn't stop at school.

What to Look For

Focus on one aspect of your writing. For example, show your child that your proposal letter or marketing plan follow a specific format and organization.

Connections to the Curriculum

- writing for a specific audience
- organization, ideas, editing, proofreading

Learn'Em Good
Idea #11

Budgeting Plan

Let's assume that your child continuously asks you for an allowance, or an increase in allowance. A great way to avoid the pestering and to help your child improve his or her writing would be to have your child find ways for the family to decrease its grocery, entertainment, or vacation budget. Tell your child that with the money saved, he or she can get an allowance (or an increase in the present allowance). Have your child write a list of expenses, and then a procedure as to how the family can save money.

What to Look For

Younger kids might have some difficulty with this so you can have them write down a plan of chores to do in order to receive an allowance. Younger students should try to persuade you (as if they already don't do that, right?) to give them an allowance. For all students, focus on the 'procedural writing'. Make sure your child writes a logical list that is coherent and organized.

Connections to the Curriculum

- writing for an intended audience
- procedural writing
- persuasive writing (younger students)
- organization

Learn'Em Good
Idea #12

Fridge Messages

Encourage your child to leave you messages on the fridge. For example, your child may have gone out to soccer practice and didn't see you after school. He or she can leave you a message on the fridge as to where he or she went, return time, etc. Older students can leave messages when they go to a friend's house or out to the mall.

What to Look For

Details, details, and more details. Have your child write *exactly* where, when, who, why and all the other details. Younger students should focus on proper letter writing (e.g. Dear Mom…) skills and some details. Older students should add more details to their notes (e.g. I'm at 32 Maple Street, the fourth house on the left).

Connections to the Curriculum

- spelling, specific vocabulary
- letter writing format
- details
- organization

Learn'Em Good
Idea #13

Rainy Days – Puppet Shows and Skits

Kids love to put on skits and perform puppet shows. There is nothing better than keeping your child occupied and learning on a rainy day. Younger kids can write out their lines and say them out loud while performing a puppet show. Older students can write a script including the both dialogue and actions. This is also perfect to do when your kids have friends over. They will become motivated to do this especially if you tell them that the parents want to watch.

What to Look For

Younger students should focus on proper grammar and punctuation. Students in grades 3-6 should pay attention to quotation marks. All students should make sure that their stories have a beginning, middle and end and, more importantly, their skit should have a problem and a solution.

Connections to the Curriculum

- grammar
- beginning, middle, end
- punctuation (quotation marks)
- problem/solution
- dialogue

Learn'Em Good
Idea #14

Pizza, Sandwiches, and Pie

A great way to spend time with your child and help him or her with writing skills is to do some cooking or baking. With your child, make a plan to cook, make, or bake his or her favorite dish. Have your child write a procedure before you make the food. You can plan this early in advance so that your child can create a shopping list to buy the items first.

What to Look For

Your child should write a proper procedure (see procedure writing in this book). Focus on the sequence. Your child's procedure should be in logical order. The introductory sentence should state exactly what is to be done.

Connections to the Curriculum

- time/order sequence
- procedure writing
- organizing ideas
- grammar

Learn'Em Good
Idea #15

Song Lyrics

If your child likes music, you can have him or her copy the lyrics of a song, change a few words, and sing it to you (or sing it alone if he or she is shy). Your child's interest for music will make this writing activity tons of fun. Young children can do this activity with simple songs like 'Mary Had a Little Lamb".

What to Look For

Your child will be practicing his or her word choice skills, vocabulary development, and thesaurus/dictionary skills. Younger students should focus on word families (e.g. double oo's like food, foot, loop). Older students can work on syllabication and dictionary skills.

Connections to the Curriculum

- spelling
- rhyming/word families
- word structure (syllables)
- dictionary/thesaurus skills
- oral communication

Learn'Em Good
Idea #16

Babysitter Instructions

This is a great way for your child to get some revenge and tell the babysitter what to do for a change. Help your child write instructions for the babysitter. Your child can combine a list of instructions with accompanying explanations (e.g. Snacks are at 8:00. Make sure David only eats…because…).

What to Look For

Focus on the organization of the instructions as they should be in chronological order. Help your child with the explanations that accompany the instructions (this isn't necessary for younger students).

Connections to the Curriculum

- procedural writing
- persuasive writing (younger students)
- organization
- paragraph writing
- developing ideas

Learn'Em Good
Idea #17

Santa, the Tooth Fairy, and the Easter Bunny

This idea doesn't require extra motivation from parents. Younger kids enjoy trying to communicate with Santa and the Tooth Fairy. This writing activity caters to a vast number of writing skills. Your child can write a persuasive piece of writing to Santa indicating why he or she should get a certain toy. Or, your child can write a recount (a retell of an event) to the Tooth Fairy of the time and place his or her tooth fell out. Furthermore, you can focus on any connection to the curriculum. I suggest that you find out what your child's teacher is working on in class (e.g. recount writing, spelling, or voice) and use the letter to Santa, the Tooth Fairy, or the Easter Bunny as reinforcement at home. Older students can write a persuasive letter to a family member as to why he or she should get the toy of his or her choice.

What to Look For

Your focus depends on what you are looking for. You can focus on a specific format (e.g. recount, persuasive), and/or skills (e.g. sentence structure, grammar, voice).

Connections to the Curriculum

- grammar, spelling
- any form of writing
- persuasive writing
- developing and organizing ideas

30

Learn'Em Good
Idea #18

Using Video Games for Writing

I have suggested this idea to many parents and it has had much success. The next time your child wants a new video game, make him work for it. You can either purchase a video game manual at your local video game store, or, you can go online to a video game site that has video game reviews. Get your child (usually a son in this situation) to read the manual or the review and then write a procedure stating how he will win at the game. This activity improves your child's reading and writing skills, and teaches him some responsibility.

What to Look For

Your child should write a proper procedure (see procedure writing in this book). Focus on the sequence. Your child's procedure should be in logical order. The introductory sentence should state exactly what is to be done.

Connections to the Curriculum

- procedure writing
- sequencing
- paragraphing
- linking/transition words
- organizing ideas

31

Learn'Em Good
Idea #19

Newspaper Headlines

Cut out some headlines from your newspaper. Try to get some funny or ambiguous headlines. Paste the headlines to a piece of lined paper and have your child write a news story that would accompany the headline. After, read the original story with your child and see how similar or different his story is to the original. Then, your child can use the reading skill of comparing and contrasting.

What to Look For

This activity is great for constructing paragraphs, time/order sequence, descriptive writing, grammar, beginning, middle and end. Focus on one or two writing skills when doing this activity.

Connections to the Curriculum

- descriptive writing
- grammar (sentence structure, punctuation)
- paragraphing
- linking/transition words
- beginning, middle, end
- developing ideas

Learn'Em Good
Idea #20

Create a Comic Strip

Have your child create a comic strip with captions (i.e. dialogue and/or narrative). Your child can create a comic strip based on a television show or movie he or she likes or your child can simply create a comic strip from scratch. When done, have your child color it in and you can post it somewhere in the house.

What to Look For

This is a good activity for younger students (grades 1-3 and even grade 4) to practice writing a beginning, middle, and end. Look for different character 'perspectives'. Older students, who are studying history in school, can create a comic based on their studies.

Connections to the Curriculum

- character perspective
- sequencing
- beginning, middle, end
- dialogue
- organizing information

33

Learn'Em Good
Idea #21

Turn Your Home into a Writing Museum

Turn your home into a text-rich environment by exposing your child to magazines, books, maps, manuals, cookbooks, menus, television guides, newspapers, fiction books, non-fiction books, dictionaries, reference books, shopping catalogues, flyers, and directories. This will give your child a much better understanding of the types of writing that are found in everyday life. They also serve as good examples and models for your child when he or she has to complete writing tasks for homework.

What to Look For

Point out to your child the structural differences, the formatting, and the styles of writing. For example, you can point out to your child how the newspaper has a headline, subheading, and body of text whereas a television guide contains the TV show and a brief summary.

Connections to the Curriculum

- identifying different types of writing
- writing for different purposes
- media literacy (format of different media texts)

Learn'Em Good
Idea #22

Faulty Toys and Misleading Products

Most parents don't realize that when their child buys a bad toy or finds out that a piece of sports equipment they just bought doesn't work well, it provides their child with a good writing situation. That is, your child can write a letter of complaint to the manufacturer. You can have your child write a formal letter to the company stating his or her dissatisfaction with the product. This is also a great opportunity for your child to use a word processor.

What to Look For

Look for proper letter writing skills (see 'Letter Writing' in the next section), grammar, punctuation, writing paragraphs, and spelling. This is a great activity for children of all ages.

Connections to the Curriculum

- grammar
- punctuation
- spelling
- letter writing
- paragraphing
- developing writing ideas

Learn'Em Good
Idea #23

Power Point Presentations

My students always have fun with this one. Your child can use power point to create personal recounts from trips, a personal narrative about him or herself, an explanation, or a procedure (the next section covers all of these types of writing). Power point is a great tool because your child can have tons, and I do mean tons, of fun creating the slide show with text. All kids from every grade can use power point slide show presentations to create any type of writing. It is also a huge confidence booster.

What to Look For

Focus on one type of writing skill (see the next section or ask your child's teacher what your child needs to improve on).

Connections to the Curriculum

- all types of writing styles
- grammar
- media literacy (creating multimedia text)
- classifying ideas
- organizing ideas

Learn'Em Good
Idea #24

Special Day Recounts

Have your child write a recount (see the next section on recounts) following his or her birthday, religious holiday, or any other special occasion. A recount is a great way for your child to express his or her feelings about the day. This activity also carries sentimental value because you can look back at it in the future.

What to Look For

Focus on the characteristics of a personal recount, specifically linking/transition words and paragraphing. Also, have your child pay attention to his or her verb tenses. The verb tenses should all be in the 'past' when writing a recount.

Connections to the Curriculum

- recount writing
- paragraphing
- linking/transition words
- proofreading and editing
- organizing ideas

Learn'Em Good
Idea #25

Movie Reviews

A parent of one of my former students used this great idea. For every fourth movie she took her child to, the mother had her son write a movie review. She had her son read movie reviews before she started this activity so that her son would have an idea of how to write one. This activity also helps improve reading skills.

What to Look For

Movie reviews clearly show you how well your child understands the story/movie. Make sure your child includes the beginning, middle, end, characters, time/order sequence problem, and solution.

Connections to the Curriculum

- characterization
- problem/solution
- time/order sequence (events)
- linking words
- organizing and classifying ideas

Learn'Em Good
Idea #26

A Biographical Gift

I plan on doing this one when my kids are a bit older. Pick a family member's birthday (grandparents are perfect for this one). Have your child create a biography about the family member and give the written biography to the family member as a birthday gift. You can give your child all the information he or she needs, or your child can interview the family member (see interviewing skills in the next section).

What to Look For

Clearly, your child should focus on linking words (see next section) and time order sequence. Your child can also focus on past tense verbs and descriptive language.

Connections to the Curriculum

- grammar (past tense verbs)
- paragraphing
- linking/transition words
- time/order sequence
- interviewing skills
- note taking
- organizing ideas

<u>Part 2</u>
All the Writing Skills and Tips You Need to Learn'Em Good

Business Letters -How to Write a Business Letter

When writing a business letter, students should realize that it is similar to writing a friendly letter. Students should consider who their audience is, what their reason is for writing the letter, and what exactly they want to say.

A business letter does differ from a friendly letter. Students should note the following differences when writing a business letter as opposed to a friendly letter.

- The greeting has a colon (:) in a business letter as opposed to a comma in a friendly letter.

- Business letters contain the writer's address and an 'inside address' which is the address of the person to whom the letter is being written.

- The closing of the business letter is not as casual as a friendly letter. In a friendly letter, we usually write "Love', or "Your Friend". In a business letter, the closing is more formal. We usually write, "Sincerely" or "Yours Truly".

- In a business letter, we put in two signatures. First, we place a handwritten signature and then a typed signature.

Capitalization Rules!

As a teacher, it is common to read a piece of writing and find numerous capitalization errors. Most students, though, are actually good with capitalizing the names of cities and proper names, it's the other 10 or so capitalization rules that students forget.

Here are some of the common and not-so-common capitalization rules:

Proper Nouns
We capitalize all proper nouns. Proper nouns name a specific person, place, thing, or idea.
For example: **New York Yankees, David, Colorado**

Proper Adjectives
We capitalize proper adjectives. Proper adjectives are formed from a proper noun.
For example: **Greek** salad, **French** onion soup, **Idaho** potato

Names of People
The names of people are capitalized. We also capitalize the initials or abbreviations that stand for those names.
For example: **Wayne Gretzky, J. Edgar Hoover**

Words Used as Names
We capitalize words such as *mother, father, grandma, and uncle* when these words are used as names.
For example:
Did **Father** say when we are going to the game?
(Father is used as a name, that is, we could use his real first name in place of the word Father).

Did your father say when we are going to the game?
(In this case, father describes someone but is not used as a name)

Titles Used with Names
Capitalize titles that are used with the names of people.
For example: **President Carter, Dr. Jones, Mayor David Smith**

Historical Events
Always capitalize the names of historical events, documents, and periods of time.
For example: **Treaty of Versailles, North American Act, Paleolithic Age**

Abbreviations
We capitalize abbreviations of titles and organizations.
For example: **M.D. (doctor), FBI (Federal Bureau of Investigation)**

Organizations
Capitalize the name of organizations and associations.
For example: **Girl Guides of America, Conservative Party**

First Words of a Sentence
We capitalize the first word of every sentence.
For example: **The boy is very nice.**

Days and Months
We capitalize the names of days of the week, months of the year, and special holidays.
For example: **Wednesday, June, Passover, Easter**

Names of Religions, Nationalities, and Languages
Capitalize the names of religions, nationalities, and languages.
For example: **Buddhist, American, Spanish (language)**

Official Names
Capitalize the names of businesses and the official names of their products.
For example: **Burger King, Colgate, Oreo**

Colons and Semicolons

Colons and semicolons are easy to use once you understand the rules.

Colons

- when a list of items is to follow
  e.g. I went to the store and bought some groceries such as: milk, butter, cheese and bread.

- after the greeting in a letter   e.g. Dear Mr. Jones:

Semicolons

- to separate two parts of a list when the individual parts include commas
  e.g. In order to do well in school you must; study on a daily basis, pay attention in class, and make sure that you seek extra help.

- to connect two parts of a compound sentence when you are not using a conjunction such as 'and' or 'but' to connect two parts
  e.g. I want to go swimming; I don't want to get my hair wet.

Like a period, a semicolon separates two independent clauses. Like a comma, a semicolon keeps the clauses connected.

Two similar clauses can be joined by a semicolon:

The studies show that sugar is bad for children; however the sugar from fruit seems to be offset by the fiber.

43

Common conjunctive adverbs such as: however, therefore, similarly, and thus can be used after a semicolon.

If one clause is independent and the other subordinate, a semi-colon will create a sentence fragment. If the clauses aren't related, they shouldn't be connected.

For example:

The studies show that sugar is bad for children. Children are getting plenty of exercise.

We do not use a semicolon:

1. Between an independent and subordinate clause.
2. Between independent clauses joined by a coordinating conjunction.
3. To introduce a list.

It is important to remember that semicolons should be used when:

1. Both clauses are **independent.**
2. The sentences **must be related.**

Clearly, colons have more definite rules whereas semicolons take a bit more practice to learn.

Commas

Commas have more functions in English grammar than any other form of punctuation. There are many ways to use the comma in writing.

You can help your child correctly learn how to use commas when writing.

- A comma is used to separate a group of three or more words in a list or series. Example: **I bought apples, cherries, and strawberries at the store.**

- Commas are used in dates to separate the day of the week, the month and date, and the year. Example: **Monday, June 5, 2003.**

- Commas are used to group three or more common words (nouns, verbs, adjectives or adverbs). Example: **I jumped, climbed, and ran at the park.**

- When proper nouns name a city and state, or a city and province, a comma goes between them.
  Example: **Toronto, Ontario   Miami, Florida**

- Commas are used to set off the name of a person directly addressed. Example: **David, stop biting your nails!**

- Commas start off introductions. The introduction can be anywhere from one word to a clause. The introduction usually states a person, time, place, fact, or condition. Example: **As you know, I am feeling fine.**

- Commas are used before a conjunction ('and' or 'but') in a sentence. Example: **She is a good runner, but she would rather swim.**

- A comma is used when writing numbers. Commas are used at every 3 digits in a number with 4 or more digits. Example: **4,682**

- Commas are used before a quotation and after words such as 'said', 'cried', and 'stated'. Example: **John said, "I'll play."**

- A sentence can start with an introduction that acts like a bridge between the last sentence and the new sentence. The introduction makes a transition between the two sentences. This is known as a transitional phrase and it always appears at the start of a sentence and is followed by a comma.

- Example: **I am a good soccer player. Therefore, I should be on this team.**

Clearly, commas have many functions in the English language. Have your child practice the variety of ways in order to see 'smoother' and improved writing.

Conducting an Interview in Order to Write a Report

Interviews provide authors with immediate firsthand information. By interviewing, your child will learn how to formulate questions, improve social skills, collect information, and write creatively.

There are several factors involved in conducting a good interview.

1. Do some research. It's important to get some information about the topic and person you will be interviewing (or, get some information about the career or the job of the person you will be interviewing).

2. Determine the best people for you to interview. For example, if you are doing a report about a specific law, find a lawyer in your community who practices that type of law. Or, let's suppose you are writing a report on a media issue. You can e-mail or call a local television or radio station.

3. Spend some quality time thinking about and writing down some good 'interview' questions. That is, make your questions thought provoking and engaging. When thinking about your questions, make sure that they will help make your report (or whatever you are producing) more factual and interesting.

4. After you have your questions, think of some backup questions. For example, your questions might lead to other questions and other issues, so, make sure you are ready.

5. Make sure you take good notes and record the interview.

6. If you quote the exact words during your interview, make sure you do just that, you must quote the 'exact words'.

7. Make sure you write a thank-you note or send an e-mail after the interview to thank the person.

Be sure you are well organized for your interview and that you have a good understanding of the piece of writing that follows (e.g. report, procedure, and exposition).

Conjunctions

Conjunctions connect words or parts of sentences. It is important for students to learn how to properly use conjunctions in their writing. Conjunctions contribute to the flow (i.e. the readability) of sentences. There are 3 main types of conjunctions: **coordinating**, **correlative**, and **subordinating**.

Coordinating Conjunctions

Coordinating conjunctions connect equal parts of sentences. That is, they connect words to words, phrases to phrases, and clauses to clauses.

For example:

<u>John</u> and <u>David</u> went to the soccer game. (noun to noun)

<u>John spent the day practicing soccer</u> and <u>doing his homework</u>. (phrase to phrase)

<u>David didn't like baseball</u>, <u>so he decided to play soccer instead</u>. (clause to clause)

Some coordinating conjunctions are: *and, or, but, for, so, nor, yet.*

Correlative Conjunctions

Correlative conjunctions also connect equal parts together. Correlative conjunctions come in *pairs* and *work together*.

For example:

Either David **or** John would play forward.

John wanted to play **both** forward **and** defense.

Some examples of correlative conjunctions are: *both-and, either-or, neither-nor, not only-but also.*

Subordinating Conjunctions
Subordinating conjunctions connect dependent or subordinate clauses with the independent or main clause. The subordinate clauses act as adverbs or nouns.

For example:

David quit baseball *because* he didn't like it.

He later realized he should have tried harder *while* he was playing.

Now he had to figure out *what position he should play next.*

1. *Because he didn't like* it answers the question *Why did David quit?* Therefore the clause is acting as an adverb.
2. *While he was playing* answered the question *when he should have tried* harder. This too is an adverb clause.
3. *What position he should play next* answers the question *what he had to figure out,* so this is a noun clause.

These clauses aren't complete sentences. They cannot stand alone! The must be connected to the main clauses. The subordinating conjunctions act as the link that connects the subordinate clauses to the main clause.

Some subordinate conjunctions are: *after, even if, where, although, because, until, as, before, when, while, as if, if, since, unless.*

Students should practice writing sentences with these three types of conjunctions so that their writing will have a smoother flow and become easier to read.

Descriptive Essay Writing

In order to write a descriptive essay, students must be able to first write descriptive words, descriptive sentences, and descriptive paragraphs. A descriptive essay can be a narrative, a personal recount, a report, or an explanation. The more description and detail that is added to a piece of writing, the more the reader will enjoy and understand the content.

Descriptive Words and Sentences

The key to writing descriptive words is to use a combination of adjectives, adverbs, and sensory words. Students should consider using colorful adjectives and adverbs when describing objects and actions.
For example, the sentence

'the *enormous and furious wave crashed down on the rocks with a thundering blast,*'

includes several adjectives and adverbs that describe the wave. This effect can also be used by younger students.

For example, "*the big wave crashed on the sharp rocks,*" is still more descriptive than just saying that "the wave hit the rocks".

Students should also incorporate 'sensory' words when writing. Sensory words are words that show the effects of the five senses. Students should combine sensory words to create sentences. For example, instead of just saying, "*I sat on the beach and heard the birds as they flew in the air,*" we can say, "*I felt the soft sand under my feet as I gazed at the seagulls gliding over the ocean*".

Descriptive Paragraphs

A descriptive paragraph should have a topic sentence and supporting sentences that contain descriptive words. The
51

paragraph should be organized in time-order sequence. It should also include adjectives, adverbs, and sensory words. The last sentence in the paragraph should conclude or summarize the entire paragraph and link back to the topic sentence.

Descriptive Essay

A descriptive essay should have an opening sentence telling what the essay is about. The body of the descriptive essay should contain the descriptive paragraphs, which in turn, contain the descriptive sentences and words. The last paragraph of the descriptive essay should summarize the body and make a conclusion about the topic paragraph.

Clearly, descriptive words lead to descriptive sentences, which lead to descriptive paragraphs that make up the descriptive essay. As your child uses more descriptive words in his or her writing and follows the format of writing an essay, you will see a definite improvement in his or her writing.

Descriptive Personal Narratives

When writing a personal narrative, it is important for students to remember to pay attention to descriptive words and personal feelings.

Students can improve their personal narratives by incorporating the following ideas:

Use the 5 Senses

The 5 senses (hearing, tasting, touching, smelling, seeing) bring a piece of writing to life. Students should remember to use descriptive adjectives and verbs that enhance the five senses. For example, instead of writing, "the girl smelled the flower", students can write, "the sweet scent of freshness from the flower glided into her nose".

Add Some Dialogue

Dialogue often gives a narrative a sense of 'life' as well. When applicable, students should try to incorporate some dialogue in order to give the writing a 'human feel'. Keep in mind, some narratives might be better off without dialogue. Students should consider whether or not a conversation (i.e. dialogue) fits in with the content.

Use Thoughts and Emotions

It is extremely important for writers to add their personal thoughts and emotions in their writing. This gives writing that 'personal' feel to it. When writing a narrative, students should try to write about a topic that they are somewhat emotional about (when I refer to 'emotional' I am referring to both positive and negative emotions). When writers feel strongly about something, whether it is positive or negative, those emotions will come out in their writing.

53

Descriptive Words

Descriptive words are the backbone for writing descriptive sentences, descriptive paragraphs, and descriptive essays.

When editing and proofreading a piece of writing, it is important to remove and change non-descriptive words to more descriptive ones.

Verbs
Verbs make sentences come alive. Verbs are action words that give movement to writing and allow the reader to visualize the action.

For example: *I was tired, so I* **walked** *to the door and* **turned** *the handle.*

We can change the verbs in this sentence so that it is becomes more descriptive by giving us a better picture.

For example: *I was exhausted, so I* **staggered** *to the door,* **squeezed** *the handle and* **twisted** *it to the right.*

Nouns
Common nouns such as *car, dog, tree,* and *man* aren't very descriptive. We can substitute these nouns with proper nouns such as *Toyota, Dalmatian, Maple,* and *Mr. Jones.* These nouns are specific and they let the reader visualize the writing more clearly.

Colorful Adjectives and Adverbs
Colorful adjectives and adverbs can make or break a piece of writing, especially a narrative. Adjectives and adverbs, also known as modifiers, can mean the difference between a non-descriptive and very descriptive piece of writing.

Example: *He walked through the forest and saw a bear.*

We can add adjectives and adverbs to paint a better picture of this scene.

He **cautiously** *walked through the* **dark** *forest and saw a* **ferocious Grizzly** *Bear.*

It is important for your child to first write his or her sentences, and then add in descriptive words. Your child should also be able to use a thesaurus. Try to purchase a child-friendly thesaurus for your child. Clearly focusing on detailed verbs, nouns, and modifiers will enhance and improve the quality of your (or your child's) writing.

Dictionary Use – Teach Your Child How to Use a Dictionary

Good old fashioned dictionaries offer more information than just the correct spelling of words. In fact, they are an underrated tool for teaching your child several language and vocabulary skills.

You can help your child learn to properly use a dictionary, and, gain some new English language skills.

- Show your child that words in a dictionary are listed alphabetically. Show your child that the guide words at the top of the page make it easy for your child to find a word. Make sure you show your child that they have to look at the first letter of the guide word, then the second letter, then third, and so on. Show your child how the guide words are related to the first and last words on the pages. This skill is a very effective tool when it comes to teaching your child how to spell.

- Show your child that the words in the dictionary have several meanings and opposite meanings. This is a great resource for teaching about antonyms, homonyms, etc...

- Teach your child about the accent marks and syllabic word division in words. This will help your child with spelling and pronunciation.

- My favorite feature about dictionaries is that they show 'usage' tips. This is a perfect learning tool for your child. That is, the dictionary shows your child *how* to use that specific word in context!

- Dictionaries also show your child word origins. This helps students to see the connections between words by focusing on prefixes and root words. Again, another great tool for vocabulary and spelling development.

Editing and Proofreading

Editing is the process that comes after students have changed and revised their main ideas in their writing. We often associate editing with grammar, punctuation, and spelling but editing and proofreading also involve 'sentences'.

It is important to check the length of sentences, sentence beginnings, and correct sentence types when editing and proofreading.

Sentence Length
It's not the best idea to consistently write short sentences throughout a piece of writing. The same goes for long sentences. It's best to mix up sentence lengths in writing. When editing and proofreading sentences, it is important to make sure that sentences are sometimes combined and sometimes split into two.

For example, we can combine sentences:

The cat meowed. The cat drank its milk.

This sentence could be combined into one sentence.

The cat meowed and then drank its milk.

Or, we can split sentences:

David rode his bike all day long then he came in for a bath so that he could be clean for bedtime.

This sentence can be split into two sentences:

David rode his bike all day long. After, he came in for a bath so that he could be clean for bedtime.

57

Sentence Beginnings

Sometimes sentences begin in the same way throughout a piece of writing. It's best to change the sentence beginnings.

For example:

I went to the store. I then asked the cashier where the toys were. I walked down the aisle and found what I was looking for.

In these sentences, the word 'I' is used too often. We can improve these sentences by changing the word 'I'.

I went to the store and asked the cashier where the toys were. While walking down the aisle, I saw what I was looking for.

Sentence Types

Make sure that your writing (or your child's writing) is free from *sentence fragments* and *run-on sentences*.

Sentence Fragment:
Thinks it is nice. (The subject is missing)
David thinks it is nice. (David, the subject, is in the sentence)

Run-on Sentence:

I had a tough day at school and when I got home I got some milk and cookies as I relaxed in front of the TV. (Punctuation is needed)

I had a tough day at school. When I got home I got some milk and cookies as I relaxed in front of the TV. (Punctuation has been added).

As you edit and proofread your child's sentences, you will improve the flow and grammatical structure of the text.

Editing and Proofreading Checklist

Have your child use the following checklist when he or she is editing a piece of writing. I suggest that your child use a different color for each editing type (e.g. punctuation in green, capitals in blue, etc...).

I checked for:

Punctuation   ____ . periods at the end of sentences
                 ____ ? question marks at the end of questions
                 ____ ! exclamation marks to show expression
                 ____ "" quotation marks around speaking parts
                 ____ , commas are used properly
                 ____ ' apostrophes are used correctly

Capitals   ____ at the beginning of each sentence
                 ____ in proper names and dates
                 ____ for the word 'I'
                 ____ my title has capital letters

Spelling   ____ spellchecker or dictionary
A good idea!   ____ I checked words with 5 or more letters

Sentences   ____ good word choice
                 ____ missing words/extra words
                 ____ no fragments or run-ons
                 ____ I properly indented the first sentence of a
                 paragraph

Elementary Grades – Writing Skills

Elementary writing has so many aspects that it is difficult to sum them all up in one article. What's unique about elementary writing as opposed to the junior and intermediate (middle) grade writing curriculum is the fact that elementary writing is more skill based whereas the latter refines those skills.

Elementary writing is a cumulative process whereby young students build upon basic skills to more complex ones.

Let's take a look at the developmental process of elementary (grades 1-3) writing so that you, as a parent, have an idea as to how your child is learning to write. Of course, you may not know exactly *what* to help your child with (although you can always go online to look at your child's state or provincial curriculum), but you can get an idea as to what to look for when your child comes home with a piece of writing. Take a look at the following to get a better idea:

- **Sentences** – This first basic skill an elementary student learns is how to write sentences. Students are first taught the <u>mechanics</u> of writing a sentence such as capitalizing the first word and adding a period. The next skill they will learn is to create different sentence types (declarative, question, exclamatory, etc...). While doing so, students will learn the appropriate punctuation for each type of sentence.

- **Classifying and Organizing** - After students learn how to write sentences, they will learn how to classify and organize the sentence according to the piece of writing. For example, students will learn how to organize a simple procedure (e.g. making a sandwich) and organize their ideas (e.g. sorting ideas through pictures or charts).

- **Research** – In the elementary grades, students will also learn how to find simple information and use that information in their writing (e.g. find information on lions and write the information in a simple report).

- **Personal Experiences and Reflections -** Students will also learn how to write a journal where they express their feelings about a subject and they will also learn how to recount events in their lives.

- **Forms –** Elementary students will also be exposed to the various forms of writing. For example, younger students will be introduced to the format of: *descriptive writing, explanations, recounts, letter writing, paragraph writing, persuasive writing, procedures, reports, and personal narratives.*

- **Style -** Students will begin to learn the basics of writing styles. These are the skills that will be developed in greater detail when students enter the junior and intermediate (middle) grades. Students will learn how to develop a writing voice, choosing descriptive verbs and adjectives, and develop sentence fluency (i.e. the readability of sentences).

By knowing what your child is learning in writing class, you will be able to monitor and help your child become a better writer.

Writing a Friendly Letter

Friendly letters are simple to create as long as students follow the correct format.

Prewriting a Friendly Letter

To Whom?

First, students must decide on the recipient of the letter. Is the letter for a friend, family member, or teacher? Students should keep this in mind before they begin to write because it will dictate the 'voice' and vocabulary of the letter.

Ideas?

Students should write down all the ideas they want to include in the letter. They should gather all the details they need. Do they want to share a story in their letter? Perhaps they want to discuss an experience. Students often describe events or daily routines in their lives within a letter. Maybe the student wants to write a letter discussing a book they have read, or a movie they have seen.

Writing

Format

1. Write a **heading** that includes your address and the date in the upper right-hand corner.

2. The **salutation** or greeting begins with the word *Dear* and is followed by the person's name and a comma (e.g. Dear David,). The salutation goes in the left-hand corner below the heading.

3. The **body** of the letter is where all the main ideas are found. The body is located on the second line below the salutation.

4. The **closing** is found two lines below the body. The first word is capitalized and is followed by a comma. Closings are usually written as, "Sincerely,", or "Yours truly,"

5. The **signature** is the name of the writer.

Revision

It is important to go over the letter and make sure that it is simple to read. Students should read the letter as if they were the recipient. They should make sure the letter is enjoyable to read.

Gathering Ideas for Writing

So now we know what we want to write our report on. We have worked hard to come up with an idea. Now what?

There are some obvious and not so obvious sources to gather information.

Obvious Sources (good for informational essays, expositions, and reports)

- Go online. Find reliable sources of information. Get information from several websites and make sure you reference your sources. An online encyclopedia is a great place to start.
- Read books and magazines. Again, make sure you cite your sources. Make sure you don't copy word for word. Write some point form notes then put them into your own words.
- Interview people in the community. Who better to talk to than a doctor if you are doing a report on the digestive system?
- Visit the museum or local science center. These places are perfect for finding reliable information.

Not So Obvious Sources (good for stories, narratives, and essays)

- Talk to friends, teachers, and family members. Get some good ideas from others.
- For narratives and stories, go people watching. Examine people's mannerisms when you are at the mall.
- A great way to get ideas for characters is to watch television and movies. Choose some characters you like and create your own character with similar traits.

Try to use as many sources as you can and you will find that you will have a great deal of information on any topic.

Gathering Ideas for a Personal Narrative

Personal narratives require some sense of introspection and reflection. You must be able to take a step back and look at your life. You should consider the following when gathering ideas for a personal narrative:

Hobbies and Interests

What are some of your hobbies or interests? Do prefer a certain sport? Perhaps you are interested in science, animals, or video games. What do you like to read about or watch on television? Is music important to you? By focusing in on an interest, you will be able to narrow down a topic. Then, when you have a topic (e.g. dogs) you can then write about your experiences with that topic.

Places You Have Visited

Where have you been? You can write a great deal about your time in the dentist's office or at the zoo. Maybe you were on a cruise or went camping in the forest. Reflect back on the activities you did, the feelings you had, and the experiences you can remember from these places.

Who Do You Spend Time With?

Think about the people who you spend time with. Who has the greatest impact on your life? Include friends, family, and role models. Reflect back to the good, bad, and special times you have had with these people. Do you immediately think about the every day events or special events with the people who are close to you?

You should take some time to write down some notes for each of the above headings. Then, you can combine their notes to write a personal narrative. For example, you can write a personal narrative about a recent family vacation to a cottage. You can include the specific place, the activities, and people who made the trip to the cottage memorable. They key here is for you to categorize your experiences, and then put them together to write a descriptive personal narrative.

Generating Essay Ideas

Students often find it difficult to develop writing ideas. Unless students are given a specific topic with specific sub-topics, students can spend a great deal of time deciding what to write about.

Good writing ideas come from many sources. It requires more than just sitting around thinking of an idea or surfing the internet. There are several ways to generate good ideas for writing.

Regardless of whether it is an essay, an informative report, or science report, good ideas will make all writing assignments stand out above the rest.

Here are some ways that you can generate good writing ideas:

- **Reflect upon personal experiences**. Have you been to specific places? Have you seen interesting things? Use your personal background knowledge and experiences in order to come up with ideas. For example, assume you have to write a report on a specific cultural aspect of a country. Which country? What cultural aspect? Perhaps your grandparents come from England and you enjoy soccer. There's an idea! You can write a report on the cultural impact of soccer on the English economy (for example). The point here is for you to find something that you can relate to. This will help you generate ideas and it might make the project more interesting.

- **Read stories, books, and magazines on a topic you are interested in.** By reading books and stories about personally interesting topics, you can get more ideas and gain different perspectives. For example, assume you like computers. You already have a good knowledge of home computers. Let's say you read a magazine story about a new kind of home computer or a new application or program. Having read the article on a topic that interests you, you've just stumbled upon a new idea for a report or essay.

- **Talk to friends and family.** Sometimes friends and family know you better than you know yourself. Assume you have no idea what to write about. Your parent or friend can remind you about something you did, somewhere you went, or some interest you have had in the past that you forgot about. Or, they might simply come up with a great idea for you. Don't be shy, ask others.

- **Go Online.** It's unbelievable how visiting one site about a topic can lead you somewhere completely different. You can get on the internet, have a specific topic in mind, and within a few minutes, find yourself reading about an interesting topic that has nothing to do with the first website you visited.

- **Create a topic web.** Let's say you are interested in cars, for example. Write the word 'car' in the middle of a blank page and circle it. Draw lines from the circle with 'cars' in it to create other words and put them in circles. The other words must have something to do with cars. For example, you may have written down the word 'Ferrari', or 'engine'. Then, from the words 'Ferrari' and 'engine', draw lines to other related words until you create a word web. By the time you get to the edge of the paper, you may have such words as 'Indy 500', or 'Solar Powered Cars'. This is a great way to generate ideas from your areas of interest.

Having good writing ideas will help your child create informative and interesting pieces of writing. Try as many methods above as you can in order to generate a good writing idea.

Good Writing – What Constitutes a Good Piece of Writing?

This is a tough question, especially since writing is graded subjectively.

As a parent, it is hard to determine if your child's writing would be considered 'good'. School boards and districts vary, and teachers' teaching experiences vary as well. There are other factors that are involved when determining the quality of a piece of writing.

By being aware of the elements of what would be considered a 'good' piece of writing; you can help your child improve his or her writing skills.

- **Mechanic needed.** Check for the simple mechanics in your child's writing. Work with your child and teach him or her how to find common mistakes such as: punctuation, spelling, grammar, and sentence structure.

- **Go online.** You can easily go online to your state or provincial government's curriculum website. Government education websites contain the 'content standards' or 'curriculum expectations' for every subject in every grade. Simply go to the 'Writing' strand, find your child's grade level, and find the specific content standard or expectation that relates to your child's piece of writing. For example, let's say your child is doing a report on whales. You can go to your government's education website and find exactly what is required of your child.

- **Paint a Picture.** Good writing contains ideas, concepts and words that are clear and descriptive. Regardless of the type of writing piece (e.g. report, personal narrative essay), your child should use descriptive words (a good thesaurus helps) that help describe and explain exactly what your child is trying to write about.

- **In the Army.** The army is a place that has order and organization. Your child's writing must be the same. Ideas should be expressed clearly. Paragraphs should be organized properly (i.e. the sentences in the paragraph as well as the position of the paragraphs in the essay), unnecessary words and sentences should be omitted, and introductions and conclusions must be in their proper places.

By making sure that your child has these writing features intact, you will definitely increase his or her chances on getting better writing grades.

Grammar Skills – All about Adjectives

Adding description to words is an important component of writing. Any word that describes a noun or a pronoun is called an 'adjective'. There are several ways to use adjectives when writing.

Here are 4 common ways to use adjectives when writing:

1. General Adjectives
Adjectives are describing words.
For example: "The brown dog ran in the yard."
Here, the noun '**dog**' is described as '**brown**'. So '**brown**' is the adjective.

2. Comparative and Superlative Adjectives
Add an '**er**' to make the adjective comparative. For example, if we add an 'er' to the adjective 'small' it becomes comparative, '**smaller**' (it is comparative because we are saying that it is smaller than something else).
Add and '**est**' to make the adjective superlative. For example, if we add an 'est' to the adjective 'small' it becomes superlative (superlative meaning the most) '**smallest**'.
If 'er' or 'est' don't sound right (such as 'beautifuler'), add the word 'most' or 'more' in front of the adjective (e.g. more beautiful)..

3. Demonstrative Adjectives
The words 'this', 'that', 'these', and 'those' are demonstrative.
For example, "**This house is very nice**'. Here, the word '**this**' modifies the word 'house'.

4. Adjective Phrases
A phrase is a group of words which has to stay together to make sense. The following is an adjective phrase:
"The bananas on the table are mine."
"**On the table**" is the adjective phrase that describes the noun '**bananas**'.

Grammar Skills – All about Adverbs

Adding description to words is an important component of writing. Any word that describes a single verb, single verbs, or a verb phrase is an 'adverb'.

Adverbs tell you *'when'*, *'where'*, *'how'*, and *'in what manner'* an action is performed. Most adverbs end in **'ly'**.

1. General Adverbs
For example: *"The cheetah ran **fast**."*
How did the cheetah run? It ran **'fast'**. So **'fast'** is the adverb.

Here are some more examples of adverbs.
*"She arrived **early**."* (when)
*"The boy played **quietly** and **energetically**."* (quietly=how)
(energetically=what manner)

2. Comparative and Superlative Adjectives
Comparative:
If we want to compare two or more people, places, or things, we add the word 'more' in front of the adverb.
Example: "The blue pen writes <u>more smoothly</u> than the black one."

Superlative:
If we want to show 'the most of all', we add the word 'most' in front of the adverb.
Example: "This pen writes the <u>most smoothly</u> of all."

3. 'Time' Adverbs
Time adverbs tell us 'when' the action takes place.
"I would like to have dinner <u>now</u> please."
"I practice piano <u>daily</u>."

4. 'Place' Adverbs
Place adverbs tell us 'where' the action takes place.

"Put the plates over <u>there</u>."
"I'd like to go <u>somewhere</u> for the day."

5. Adverb Phrases
A phrase is a group of words which has to stay together to make sense. Adverb phrases describe verbs or verb phrases.
"The plate on the table fell <u>to the floor</u>."

Fell where? It fell (fell is the verb or action word) <u>to the floor</u>. So, **'to the floor'** is the adverb phrase because it describes 'where' the plate fell.

"I was late when I arrived <u>at school</u>."
Arrived where? I arrived (arrive is an action word) <u>at school</u>. So, **'at school'** is the adverb phrase because it describes 'where' I arrived.

6. Manner Adverbs
Manner adverbs tell us 'in what manner' the action takes place.
"The cat moved <u>gracefully</u>."
Moved how?
The cat moved (moved is the verb or action word) <u>gracefully</u>. So, **'gracefully'** describes the manner of the movement.

Grammar Skills – All about Pronouns

Pronouns replace nouns or other pronouns. Some examples of pronouns are: 'me', 'you', 'him', 'her', 'them', and 'it'.

There are several ways to use pronouns when writing. There are several types of pronouns: personal pronouns, indefinite pronouns, possessive pronouns, and demonstrative pronouns.

1. Personal Pronouns (Objective and Subjective)
<u>Subjective</u> pronouns suggest that the pronoun is the <u>subject</u> of a sentence. Subjective personal pronouns are: *I, you, he, she, we, it, you,* and *they.*

For example:
I am happy that you came over.
You are my best friend.
Is **she** your sister?
We will be home after dinner.

<u>Objective</u> pronouns suggest that the pronoun is the object of a verb or preposition. Objective pronouns are: *me, you, her, him, it, us, you,* and *them.*

For example:

Make sure that she tells **you** the directions.
Alan should pass the ball to **him** during the game.
Did you invite **them** to your party?

2. Indefinite Pronouns
Indefinite pronouns are pronouns that refer to a general and not specific thing or person. Indefinite pronouns refer to the ideas of all, any, or some (hence not definite). Some common indefinite pronouns are: all, any, anybody, each, everybody, everyone, few, many, nobody, none, some, and somebody.

73

For example:
Did you buy **some** candy from the store?
I hope **somebody** will help me carry these.
There is **nobody** home right now.

3. Possessive Pronouns

<u>Possessive</u> pronouns suggest that the pronoun is showing the possession of one who owns an object or person. The possessive pronouns are: *mine, yours, his, hers, its, ours, yours,* and *theirs.*

For example:
The new bike is **mine**.
His hockey stick is brand new.
That cool remote control car is **ours**.

4. Demonstrative Pronouns

<u>Demonstrative</u> pronouns identify and point out a noun or pronoun. The demonstrative pronouns are: this, these, that, and those.

For example:
Those running shoes are mine.
Do you know who **those** belong to?
I brought **that** with me because I was cold.

Grammar Skills – All about Nouns

We all remember from school that a noun is a person, place, or thing.

I bet you forgot that there many types of nouns!

Nouns are usually the first parts of speech that students learn because they are concrete and students can easily visualize nouns. Younger students also learn the proper spellings of nouns because nouns can be associated with pictures. As students move to higher grades, they learn that there are several types of nouns.

Your child can improve his or her writing by being familiar with the different types of nouns. Whether your child is writing a sentence, report, or personal narrative, he/she must know the different forms of nouns.

Proper Nouns
Proper nouns represent a specific person, place, or thing. Proper nouns always begin with a capital letter. Some proper nouns are: days of the week, names of people, organizations, countries, and religions.

Common Nouns
Common nouns refer to a *general* person, place, or thing. Common nouns only begin with a capital letter when they start a sentence. Some examples of common nouns are: dog, man, and car.

Abstract Nouns
Abstract nouns are words that you cannot see, touch, feel, taste, or smell. Some examples of abstract nouns are: crime, happiness, and evolution. Notice how these examples are also common nouns. The word Judaism is a proper and abstract noun.

Concrete Nouns

Concrete nouns are the opposite of abstract nouns. Concrete nouns are words that you can see, touch, feel, taste, and smell. Some examples of concrete nouns are: house, shoe, and tree. Notice that these examples are also common nouns. My friend 'David' is a proper and concrete noun.

Collective Nouns

Collective nouns are names of groups of people, animals, or things. Some examples of collective nouns are: herd, class, and tribe.

Plural Nouns

Plural nouns indicate that there is more than one person, places, or things. For example: boys, countries, dogs.

Possessive Nouns

Possessive nouns indicate possession and usually have an apostrophe and an 's'. For example: David's, the dog's bone.

Irregular Nouns

Irregular nouns are nouns that are in plural form but do not have an 's' at the end. For example: wolf=wolves, life=lives.

Understanding the various types of nouns will help your child in any writing assignment in school because the writing will be more descriptive and detailed.

Grammar Skills – All about Verbs

The verb is an important part of English grammar. Verbs are the 'action' or 'doing' part of the sentence. Verbs bring English writing to life! Verbs create movement, action, emotion, and a dynamic feel.

There are several types of verbs that are used in English grammar. Some of the more popular English verbs are: **linking verbs, helping verbs, and compound verbs**.

1. **Linking Verbs**
    Linking verbs don't necessarily show an action. Instead, they 'link' the subject of the sentence with an object or other additional information.
    For example:
    The baseball game **was** *very good.*

    'Was' is the linking verb because it connects the <u>game</u> (subject) with being <u>good</u> (the additional information).

    Another example; *She* **seems** *nice.*
    she = subject, seems=linking verb, nice = additional information

    Some well known linking English verbs are: am, is, was, has been, becomes, will become, has become, seems, seemed, will seem, etc…

    Notice how linking verbs appear in past, present, and future tenses of the verbs 'to be', 'to become', and 'to seem'.

2. **Helping Verbs (Auxiliary Verbs)**
    Helping verbs are verbs that help main verbs express tense. There are 23 helping verbs that belong to the following main verbs: **to be, to do, to have, may, can, and would**

are just a few examples.
Helping verbs express tense.

For example;
'*He **is** laughing*' contains the helping verb 'is'.
The 'is' shows us that the action is taking place in present tense.

If we change 'He is laughing' to 'He was laughing', the tense changes. The new helping verb 'was' changes the tense of the main verb, laughing.

Some helping verbs in English grammar are: be, are, do, can, could, may, might, should, will, etc…

3. **Compound Verbs**
   Compound verbs are created by combining a helping verb and another verb.

   For example,
   *She **will go** to the movies tonight.*
   'Will' is the helping verb that 'helps' the verb 'go'.

How to Plan a Story

Many children love writing stories. From fantasy, to historical fiction, students enjoy the creativity and self expression that writing a narrative story can offer.

Quite often, students just jump in or write a brief outline before writing their narrative. The problem is that their story doesn't really have a direction and they get lost. Students should have a good plan, but before they can do so, they should have the key elements of the story in their heads first.

It is important that students spend time to 'think' about the characters, plot, and setting before writing their story.

You can help your child write a better narrative story by focusing on the following:

Characters

- Are the characters **believable**? Even in a fantasy narrative, readers must be able to identify with the characters' actions and thoughts.

- What is the main character's **problem**? The main character must have a problem and goal in the story.

- Who does the main character represent? If the story is meant for 10 year olds, the main character should be close in age.

- Who is the bad guy? The bad guy, also called the antagonist, should be clearly 'bad' and pose a problem for the main character, who is also called the protagonist.

Plot

- Main problem. What is the **main problem**? Make sure the readers know from the start what the problem is and how it is going to be solved.
- **Beginning, middle, end**? Make sure you have a beginning, middle, and end. Make sure to write an outline with several parts for each of the beginning, middle, and end.
- **Inspiration**? Try to write your plot by thinking of other books or movies. You can combine plots from movies or books to create your own unique plot.

Setting

- How many places? Make sure your story takes place in several places. Change up the locations; for example, make the story take place indoors, outdoors, and in unique and special places.
- Familiar settings? Think of places you have been to, have seen in a movie or TV, or read about.

Ask your child these questions before writing a narrative story. Your child should write a well detailed outline before starting to write his or her story. These questions will help your child start to think in the 'write' direction.

How to Write a Conclusion

Writing a conclusion is similar to writing a paragraph.

The first sentence in a conclusion is the topic sentence. It should be the most important sentence in your conclusion. Your first sentence in your conclusion must contain the main idea of your entire report.

The following sentence in your conclusion reiterates the main ideas from each paragraph. Your introduction 'introduced' your main ideas that were stated in your paragraph and your conclusion reiterates those main ideas. Essentially, you have (hopefully) given proof for your main ideas in your paragraphs, so, you can confidently state the ideas again as fact in your conclusion.

Your conclusion should be written in the following order:

1. Your first sentence must state the main idea of your entire piece of work.
2. The next few sentences should support your main idea by reiterating the main ideas from each paragraph.
3. The last sentence should be similar to the first sentence except that it should be in your own words. It should be **your** summary of the conclusion. For example, let's say you did a report on sharks. If your first sentence in the conclusion stated, "Sharks are efficient predators." your last sentence can be something like, "Sharks are clearly the king of the ocean." This sentence supports that fact that sharks are efficient predators because it states their superiority as a species.

It is important to remember to organize your concluding paragraph much like any other paragraph.

How to Write a Paragraph

It is important that your child organize all writing assignments in school and at home. Writing assignments should be organized according to their specific audience. Procedures, reports, and personal recounts all have different formats. You can help your child to organize his or her writing.

1. Make sure your child knows how to create a topic sentence that introduces the topic. Topic sentences can introduce a paragraph and an entire assignment.

2. Make sure your child understands the basic structure of a paragraph. Since a group of paragraphs make an entire writing assignment, it is important that your child understands the parts that make up the whole.

3. Help your child create 'ideas' about a topic and show your child how to organize those 'ideas' in logical order.

4. Have your child practice writing a procedure. Procedure writing is a great tool to teach students written organization because they require a logical and chronological format.

5. Provide your child with graphic organizers (such as flow charts and brainstorming webs) that allow your child to 'see' the topics on paper. Once your child 'sees' the topics, he or she can start to organize them.

6. Use a word processing program such as Microsoft Office. Your child will be able to separate paragraphs and move them around at will (as opposed to writing the work on paper). This will give your child more flexibility to practice organizing and reorganizing his/her writing.

Ideas – Writing Ideas for Various Writing Genres

Writing ideas are sometimes hard to come by. It is easy for most students to start to find information, but it is difficult for them to decide on an idea unless they are given a specific one from their teacher.

Students should choose a topic based on the type of writing assignment. For example, a topic for a report is quite different than that of an explanation.

The following 5 types of writing each have their own unique topics. They are:

- Explanatory
- Persuasive
- Descriptive
- Narrative
- Procedural

Explanatory

- **Causes** - volcanoes, erosion, hatred, tornadoes, pollution, war
- **Different Kinds of...** - movies, stores, cities, clothes, music, TV shows, villains
- **Definitions** - family, fear, friends, culture

Persuasive

- **Persuading** - homework is bad, stealing is wrong, seat belts, too much TV, video games are fun, gum should be allowed in school, pets should have rights

Descriptive

- **Places** - your home, city, country, zoo, forest, store, kitchen, lake, farm
- **People** - friend, teacher, hero, family member, famous athlete, singer, actor
- **Things** - pet, bicycle, video game, car, food, book, hobby

Narrative

- **Fiction** - fantasy story, historical fiction, romance, science fiction, realistic fiction,
- **Essay** - being happy, being a good friend, learning, volunteering

Procedural

- **How to...** - bake a cake, exercise, save money, how to vote, fix something, teach something, take care of a pet

Of course, there are many, many more ideas out there for each category. What's important for students though, is to choose (if they are able to) a topic which they are interested in, then, they can decide on the type of writing. Or, if a student is required to do a type of writing (e.g. an explanation), then they can decide upon a topic of interest.

Improving Writing through Conventions

What are conventions?

Conventions are the fancy educational word for the 'mechanical' correctness of writing.

This refers to the proper spelling, paragraphing, the use of capitals, punctuation, and overall grammatical structure (pretty much everything besides the actual content).

A good piece of writing consists of two major components. The first is obviously the content of the work (i.e. the message, the story, or the facts). The second is the structure of the writing (i.e. the conventions). Students can improve their writing skills (specifically regarding conventions) through practice. They must consistently proofread and edit their writing with care (and not rely so much on a word processing program). Since the improper use of conventions disrupts the flow of the writing, it thus has an effect on the message (which we know is part of the content).

After your child writes his/her rough draft of a piece of writing, review the following tips in order to check for the correct use of conventions.

- Make sure spelling is correct. Students shouldn't completely rely on word processors because word processors do not always take in account the 'context' of the word (therefore the word processor might give a homonym, which may be the incorrect word in the particular context).

- Students should have a thorough understanding of the rules of capitalization, quotation marks, grammar, and paragraphing.

- Make sure that your child's writing conventions are at grade level (you can easily go online to see the curriculum standards for your child...simply search for your child's state/province and 'curriculum').

- Give your child an editing checklist and have him/her choose 1 convention at a time to check. For example, assume your child is ready to edit. Have him/her start off using a green pen or pencil crayon to check all capitals. Then, use a blue pen or pencil to correct all spelling mistakes, and so on. It is important to use different colors compartmentalize each convention when making corrections.

You can use these strategies to help develop your child's writing skills and improve his/her use of conventions.

Improving Writing through Grammar

It is easy for a student to correct his or her writing, granted he or she knows where the mistakes are.

I have seen it over and over in my classrooms; students editing their writing but still missing their mistakes! As adults, we can correct our mistakes because we know how to use a dictionary properly, we can hear the 'flow' of our sentences, and we know how to use spell checkers. But for some students, it's a different story.

Children must learn *how to look for errors* and be shown *how to recognize them*!

Here are some techniques that you can impart to your child. Keep in mind, these are <u>skills</u> and they must be practiced consistently when writing.

- Have your child use **automatic spell check** when using a word processing program. Automatic spell checking underlines misspelled words in red. This is the first step towards your child 'noticing' spelling mistakes.

- Teach your child how to use a **dictionary**. I've tutored grade 5 students who do not know how to use a dictionary properly. Not only will these skills help students find misspelled words, but it will also help improve their spelling a great deal.

- Have your child learn the different **homophones** (e.g. their and there, your and you're…). Misused homophones are extremely common. A good grasp of the various homo-phones is important for effective writing.

- **Sentence structure** skills should be practiced. Run-on sentences and sentence fragments are common elements in poor writing. Have your child avoid these nuisances that hinder good writing.

- **Punctuation!** Your child should be well versed in the use of commas, quotation marks, exclamation marks, question marks, etc… If your child has difficulties with punctuation, find an online 'editing checklist' (or get one from the teacher) which will help your child look for each type of punctuation to correct.

Again, the above are all skills that must be learned over time. Focus on one skill and when you see that your child has mastered it, move on to the next.

Informational Essays and Reports

An essay is a form of factual writing that is more than one paragraph in length. The key to writing a good informational essay or report is to be organized and understand the process and structure.

Prewriting

<u>Starting Off</u>

Before writing an informational essay, it is important to plan the 'who', 'what', and 'why'.

- It is important to know who or what you are writing about. Unless you are given a specific topic to write about, it is important to choose a topic that really interests you. If you are given a topic that does not necessarily interest you, find out if you can cover a subtopic or a topic related to the one that was given to you.

- Know who will be reading your report/essay. Will it be for your classmates, teacher, or community?
  Your vocabulary, facts, and overall writing should be dictated by your audience. That is, you wouldn't want to include difficult scientific concepts and vocabulary if your essay is to be read by other students.

- Lastly, how do you want your writing to sound? Do you want the essay to be very serious, funny, or scientific? The 'way' you write is sometimes just as important as 'what' you write. Your message will be understood according to the tone in your writing.

Putting it Together

What type of information do you plan on using? First, find reliable sources and determine important information. Once you have your information, find a focus. That is, specifically what aspect of the topic do you want to focus on? Then, organize your information into sub-categories. The rule of thumb is to use 3 main ideas in your essay and focus on each idea within their own paragraphs.

The 1st Draft

Remember, a good essay, like a story, must have a beginning, middle, and end.

Beginning
Your introductory paragraph should say something interesting or surprising in order to get the reader's attention. It should also introduce the subtopics you will be discussing in your essay.

Middle
The middle should include all of the ideas, facts, examples, and information about your topic. Each paragraph should contain a separate sub-topic and should be properly organized.

End
The final paragraph, or conclusion, should summarize the main points covered in your informational essay/report. It should also remind the reader what your main ideas were and why they were important.

Revising and Editing

Make sure that you have done the following in order to edit your writing:

1. Does my title identify my topic?

2. Have I introduced my topic in my introduction? Is my introduction interesting?
3. Are my paragraphs well organized (i.e. topic sentence, supporting sentences)?
4. Have I included facts, proof, and information that support my topic?
5. Will readers understand my writing (i.e. have I written to the correct audience)?
6. Have I edited my writing (i.e. grammar, punctuation, sentences)?

By staying organized and following the structure of an information essay/report, you will improve your chances for writing a well written essay.

Letter Writing

In the primary grades (1-3) students are introduced to writing a friendly letter.

You can help your child write a friendly letter by focusing on prewriting, writing, and editing techniques.

1. **Prewriting** - Your child should choose a recipient (unless they are already given one by their teacher). He/she should choose someone they feel comfortable with so that he or she will not feel shy and write more freely. Have your child gather all the ideas required for a letter.

Your child can write about the following:

- describe a personal event or accomplishment
- tell about a recent book, movie, or magazine
- share a story of a situation
- ask questions to find out how the recipient is doing

2. **Writing** - Your child should begin by writing a paragraph for each idea on their list. If your child is only writing about one idea, he/she should break down the idea into sub-topics. For example, let's say your child wants to write about a certain event that happened on the weekend. Your child can write about the events leading up to the situation, the situation itself, and what happened after the situation.

3. **Editing** - Your child should check for punctuation, spelling, capitalization, and overall format of the letter. Have your child check over each of these separately. That is, don't have your child start reading and look for spelling, punctuation, and capitalization at the same time. This is overwhelming! Start off with spelling, for example, and then edit the others.

Linking and Transition Words

Sentences and paragraphs must be organized so that the reader can easily follow the information from one sentence to the next, and more importantly, from one paragraph to the next.

Transition, or linking words, allow writers to connect sentences and paragraphs. Transition or linking words can indicate the **time order**, **place order**, and **order of importance**.

Time Order

When writing, it is extremely important to indicate the chronological (time) order of events otherwise the reader will be confused as to when everything happened.

Some **time order** linking words are:

about, after, before, during, first, second, third, today, tomorrow, yesterday, next, soon, after, finally, then, and *as soon as*

Place Order

When writing a descriptive or expository paragraph or essay, students should use place order linking words. Place order linking words describe where things are located.

Some **place order** linking words are:

above, across, along, around, behind, below, beside, between, by, down, in front of, in back of, inside, outside, near, over, left, right, under

Order of Importance

News stories and essays should be organized in order of importance. That is, the most important information should be given first. Students should use this concept when writing persuasive and expository essays. Sometimes, writers like to save the most important point for last as well.

Some **order of importance** words are:

for this reason, in fact, for instance, as a result, therefore, in conclusion, firstly, most importantly, secondly, on the other hand, however, in summary,

Students should use these linking words to begin a paragraph and sentence when writing.

More on Transition Words

In a personal narrative or recount, the reader has to know when things happen and in what order. Understanding the order of events helps the reader organize the information.

Transition words help the reader know the time order of events in a piece of writing. Some examples of transition words are: during, after, next, then, and before.

It is important for writers to use transition words not only to show the time order, but to separate the events. The transition words help the reader break up the events so that they are not meshed together.

Your child can use the following writing cues in order to practice time order and transition words for longer pieces of writing (e.g. personal narratives and recounts).

- Your child can write a sentence that could be from one of his/her personal narratives. Your child can replace a word with a transition word at the beginning of the sentence.

- Your child can write a sentence about a recent experience and use a transition word to start it off.

- Your child can write two sentences using a transition word to connect the two ideas. The second idea should begin with a transition word.

- Your child can practice using transition words by writing a retell of his/her day (not all the details from the day are needed, only a handful of main events). The retell should include several transition words that connect the events in time order.

My Child Doesn't Like to Write

It isn't easy to motivate students to write if they are not interested. Quite often, unmotivated students see writing as a chore as opposed to a form of self expression.

They key to motivating your child to write is to focus on the content as opposed to the form. If you can get your child interested in writing for the sake of writing, he/she will ultimately develop the appropriate skills later on.

You can help motivate your child to write by trying some of the following:

1. Reward your child for completing any writing activities whether it is at school or at home. Rewards such as praise, movie, or extra video or TV time are good ideas. You know your child best.

2. Have your child create personal stories about topics of interest. For example, if your child likes a certain movie, sport, video game, or TV show, have him/her write a story about his or her topic of interest. Your child can include him or herself in the story. Let your child make it silly, funny, or any way (within reason) he or she wishes. Your child is more likely to try to be successful when writing about something of interest.

3. Encourage your child to read his or her stories to family members. There's nothing like positive reinforcement, encouragement, and praise from loved ones. Your child will develop a sense of pride and accomplishment.

4. My favorite suggestion is to have your child type out his/her story on the computer (or a family member can do the typing if it is difficult for the child). Your child can learn how to use spell check, and, for added story writing fun, your child can paste pictures into a program such as Microsoft PowerPoint to make a slide show to accompany his or her story. This is a great way to

get your child interested in writing. He/she will have a slide show (which is like a movie) that will give him/her a visual representation of the story.
This is great when your child writes about anything from superheroes to science fiction stories.

Wait until your child has developed an interest in writing until you decide to work on his/her writing skills. Once your child begins writing on a regular basis, you will have overcome the motivation issue and could then begin working on writing skills.

Parentheses

We use parentheses three ways in writing.

1. **To Show Less Important Information** – We use parentheses in writing when we want to show that something is of less significance than something else.

   For example: *My friend David (who is short) came over to play hockey.*

   Here we can clearly see that the main idea of the sentence was that David was the friend of the speaker. The fact that David was short was of less importance to the main idea of the sentence. This idea that David is short also shows digression from the main idea.

2. **Numbers in a List** – We can write a list by using commas but when we number the items in the list, we must use parentheses.

   For example, a list with commas:
   I am going to buy milk, bread, and butter at the store.

   For example, a numbered list with parentheses:
   I am going to buy (1) milk, (2) bread, and (3) butter at the store.

The main idea here is that if the list is going to be numbered, parentheses are needed. Numbers are used when describing order.

3. **Citation** – We use parentheses when citing written work.

   For example:

   The war began because "both sides were being funded by the same bankers" (Smith 1998).

Personal Narratives

A personal narrative, or recount, is a true story about something that happened to the person who is writing, hence, it is personal writing.

The following description will help you help your child write a personal piece of writing.

A personal writing piece is the retelling or recounting of someone's past experiences. They are usually told in the first person "I". Personal writing is descriptive accounts with details that support the writer's perspective. It is also important to know that personal writing is structured in a chronological order. The focus of the personal writing piece is to create sequential events that involve the author. There are several types of personal writing such as, personal recounts, autobiographies, letters, diaries, eye-witness accounts, and journals.

Personally written narratives usually begin with an opening statement that introduces the 5w's (who, what, where, when, why). The important events are discussed in detail throughout the body in paragraphs. Each paragraph should discuss a particular event. The beginning of each paragraph should start with a linking word such as: first, after, soon, when, later, or finally. The last part of the personal narrative should include a concluding statement. This concluding statement should sum up the author's summary of the events.

The personal writing piece should also have the proper language conventions. The participants in the recount should be as specific as possible (e.g. instead of my aunt, it should be my Aunt Jenny). Recounts should also be written in past tense. Students should edit their work by paying attention to their verb tenses. Linking words that clearly illustrate the chronology should be used. Details and a first person perspective are also essential for a well written personal narrative.

Persuasive Expositions

The purpose of persuasive writing (or an exposition) is to create ideas and support them with proof in order to present a logical argument with a point of view.

An exposition must have the following in correct order:

1. An introductory paragraph stating the topic, problem, and point of view.
2. A paragraph that supports the author's point of view.
3. A paragraph that goes against the author's point of view.
4. An evaluation or summary that reiterates the author's point of view.

Some examples of persuasive writing are:
Do video games promote violence in young people?
Should schools have vending machines?
All animals should be micro chipped.

Expositions (persuasive writing) should persuade readers to agree with a writer's particular point of view. It must compare or contrast issues that will persuade the reader that the author's point of view is correct. Finally, the writing should present all points in order to form a logical conclusion based on the information and proof given by the writer.

Students must make sure that they:
- Start their opinion clearly.
- Gave strong reasons to support their opinion.
- Organized their reasons in logical order.
- Presented both sides of the argument.
- Clearly indicate what they want the readers to think regarding the issue.

Planning a Paragraph

It is important to plan a paragraph because a combination of good paragraphs is the backbone for a good piece of writing.

Make a Plan
Before writing a paragraph, it is important to determine the bigger picture.

1. First determine what the topic of the paragraph will be. The rest of the paragraph will support the topic sentence.

2. Who is the audience? Will a teacher or other students be reading the paragraph? The paragraph should be consistent with the rest of the writing. It should be more complex for adult readers and simpler for younger readers.

3. What is the form? Determine what type of paragraph it will be (i.e. factual, narrative?).

Get the Information

It is time to gather all the details for the paragraph. The topic sentence must introduce the idea of the paragraph and the supporting sentence must support the topic.

Descriptive paragraphs - should have details that focus on the five senses (i.e. focus on adjectives and descriptive words)

Narrative paragraphs - should contain details about an experience and problems in sequential order

Persuasive paragraphs - must contain facts, figures and proof to back up your opinion

Expository paragraphs - have facts to explain a process or

phenomenon

Organize

Make sure the topic sentence of the paragraph is first. Next, make sure the supporting sentences give proof, facts, or information that supports the topic sentence. The last sentence is the closing sentence. This sentence sums up the paragraph.

Editing

Read your paragraph out loud. Make sure you have a good introduction, supporting details, and your conclusion. Check spelling, punctuation, and sentence structure.

Remember, good paragraphs lead to good reports and essays.

Printing Neatly - Help My Child Print Neatly (Part 1)

Neater printing comes in due time, it's just a matter of practice.

You can help your child print neatly by practicing at home. Try to follow some of these steps to help your child print or write neatly.

1. First, have your child place his or her fingers to create a space between words. The rule of thumb (no pun intended) is to have one finger space between words.

2. Make sure your child tilts the paper (right handed person should tilt paper to left and vice versa).

3. Purchase printing practice workbooks at your local educational store. These are small booklets with letters already placed in the correct position on the line. Your child will be able to trace words and letters, and then write them on his or her own.

4. Teach your child to look at the next word to determine if there is enough space at the end of the page or if he/she should start writing on the next line.

5. Get some graph paper (graph paper is covered with squares instead of lines for writing). Have your child print letters in the blocks (one letter per block) and skip a block when writing a new word. This will give your child a sense of consistent spacing.

Watch your child print or write. Gently correct your child if you see any deviations from neatness.

Printing Neatly – Help My Child Print Neatly (Part 2)

When we think of a student who has difficulty writing neatly the first thing that enters our minds is eye hand coordination. We assume that he/she has a psychomotor problem.

While this may sometimes be the case, there are some other factors which explain why a child does not print neatly.

One such explanation is 'spacing'. Spacing refers to the spaces (obviously) between both words and sentences.

Before trying the following tips, have your child's vision checked by a professional.

1. Make sure your child is sitting upright and with the paper slightly tilted (try writing on a straight piece of paper, it's very awkward!).

2. When printing, have your child place little dots between letters and a small finger space between words. This will show your child the correct spacing between both words and letters.

3. Try to show your child examples of handwritten work for your child to use as reference when printing.

4. Teach your child to always look at the next word to determine if there is enough space before the margin.

5. If your child's writing is really messy, get some graph paper (squared paper) and show him/her to write letters in each block. You can also show your child to skip blocks between words.

Have your child practice these skills on a regular basis. It will be just a matter of time until your child is printing neatly.

Procedure Writing

There is actually a procedure to writing procedures!

Writing a procedure is a great way for students to practice organization and detail writing skills. In order to write a procedure, students will learn how to write text that follows a pattern by listing steps that show how to do something.

Procedures are usually associated with writing science experiments. They also include recipes and 'how to' manuals. Students can write a procedure in science, social studies, and math.

You can help your child organize a procedure by following these steps (I guess you can say that this is also a procedure). Each of the following should be in its own paragraph.

1. Your child should list the 'goal or aim' of the procedure. This is an outline of what is to be done.

2. Then, your child should include any materials, instruments, or ingredients needed for the procedure.

3. The method is the most important part of the procedure. The method is a list of steps, either in list form or in paragraphs.

4. The last part of a procedure is the evaluation. The evaluation states whether or not the goal was achieved.

Your child should use linking words that illustrate a chronological order. The procedure should also be written in present tense and towards a general audience.

Punctuation – Question Marks and Exclamation Points

All sentences end in some form of punctuation. A question mark always follows a direct question. An exclamation point always conveys strong emotions.

Question Marks
Question marks are always part of a direct question. There are three types of questions.

1. **Indirect Questions:** There are no question marks in indirect questions. There are no quotations and there is no one actually asking a question.
    For example: *Mike asked who wanted to play soccer.*

2. **Direct Questions**: Direct questions involve somebody speaking. Quotation marks are used in direct quotations.
    For example: *"Who wants to play soccer?" Mike asked.*

3. **Series Questions:** With series questions, each question can be followed by a question mark.
    For example: *Do you want to play soccer? Would you rather play baseball? Would you rather watch us play?*

Exclamation Points
An exclamation, which can be a word, phrase, or clause, is an expression of strong emotions or commands.
For example:
That was the best movie I ever saw!
"Watch out!" David shouted as the piano fell from the building.
In the second sentence, the exclamation point is inside the quotation marks because David yelled 'watch out'.

Exclamation points shouldn't be used too much in writing because they can lose their sense of strong emotion if there are too many of them.

Quotation Marks

In order for students to properly write narratives, they must know the rules of using quotation marks.

Quotation marks are used to enclose the exact words of the person speaking. Quotation marks also show that words are used in special ways, as well; they are used to punctuate titles.

Direct Quotations

Quotation marks are placed before and after the spoken words. For example,

"David is a very nice guy," Emma said.

Notice how the quotation marks are exactly around the words that Emma said. Also, notice how the comma after the word 'guy' is *inside* the quotation marks.

Special Words

Quotation marks are used to separate a word that is being discussed.

For example,

The word "said" is used to often in writing.

The word 'said' is not actually being spoken, it is being set apart from the rest of the sentence (I actually did it in this sentence).

Punctuate Titles

Quotation marks are used to punctuate the titles of songs, short stories, book chapters, magazine and newspaper articles, and poems.

For example,

"O Canada" (Song – National Anthem)
"Escape" (Book Chapter)

Commas, Periods, and Quotation Marks

Exclamation and question marks are placed inside the quotation marks when it punctuates the quotation. They are placed outside when it punctuates the main sentence.

For example,

"Do you want to go with me to the toy store?" asked mom.
In this sentence, the question mark is inside the quotation marks because the question mark is punctuating the words inside the quotation.

"Yes for sure!" I replied
Again, the exclamation is punctuating the words inside the quotation.

Did the daughter say, "I want to go to"?
In this sentence, the question mark is not just referring to the words 'I want to go to". The question mark refers to 'Did the daughter say, "I want to go to"?', therefore; the question mark punctuates the main sentence.

Understanding the proper use of quotation marks is an essential skill for properly writing dialogue.

Report Writing

A report is a factual piece of writing that contains information. Reports involve research to explore a topic.

The key behind writing a good report is to be well organized. Students must learn to organize their ideas and present them in a clear and succinct.

If your child is writing a report, you can help him/her organize it effectively at home.

1. Have your child choose a specific topic for the report (granted your child has a choice).

2. Your child should decide on 3-5 main ideas to focus on. For example, if your child is doing a report on elephants, he can focus on: 1) Appearance, 2) Diet, 3) Babies, 4) Behaviors.

3. Have your child find information on each of the 3-5 main ideas. He/she can write the information in point form notes. Make sure your child focuses on facts, data, and good detailed information. If needed, your child can organize the information in a graphic organizer.

4. Now, your child has enough information to write 3-5 paragraphs. Help your child to write a topic sentence for each paragraph. The topic sentences should introduce the paragraph's content. Then, he can take his point form notes and put them together in sentences.

5. After your child has the 3-5 paragraphs with good topic sentences, he/she should write a good, strong opening that tells the main idea of the report. A good opening can be a question or very interesting fact. A strong opening sentence makes the reader want to read on.

6. A strong closing sentence or sentences finishes off the report. The closing should sum up the report and connect the main ideas together. It's almost like a summary of the report.

7. Finally, the fun part. Edit, edit, and edit. Have your child use an editing checklist.

8. When your child is finished, allow him/her to read the report out loud to family and/or friends.

Clearly, writing a report is not difficult once your child learns the proper organization and format. It is important for your child to add in facts and details. A report must have good factual information for the reader.

Revising

It is important for students to learn how to correctly revise their work before handing it in. Revision includes correcting grammar, spelling, and content.

You can easily help your child learn to revise his or her writing.

Organization
Make sure that the topic sentences and paragraphs are organized accordingly. If the topic sentence or introduction contains, ideas a, b, and c, then the paragraphs should be organized in the same order (i.e. a, b, and c). Perhaps some paragraphs have to be reordered if they are not organized accordingly.

Ideas
Go over the main ideas that are presented. Make sure that all the important points are expressed. If the writing is an opinion or persuasive, make sure that both sides of the argument are presented.

Strengths
Start off by underlining or putting a note beside the sentences or paragraphs that demonstrate good writing. This will make the rest of the revision less painful.

Weaknesses
Focus on one aspect of revision at a time. For example, start off looking for missing details, then work on grammar, and then focus on sentence structure etc...

Read Out Loud
By far, the best way to revise writing is to read it out loud. This is the best method to catch mistakes than weren't caught when reading silently.

111

Information

Should more information be added? Make sure the topic sentences state the main idea and make sure that the rest of the paragraph contains the supporting details. Also, make sure that the concluding statement supports the topic sentence. Are facts or data required? Don't be shy to delete or cross out any irrelevant information and make sure that there isn't too much repetition.

Show, Don't Tell

Use the 5 senses to add description to a piece of writing. Try not to use a 'passive' voice. Instead, use an 'active' voice. Verbs are good words to use because they add more 'movement' to a piece of writing.

Detail, Detail, Detail

Check for detail, especially when writing a narrative. Make sure that the reader definitely knows exactly what is being referred to when they read such words as 'they', 'him', 'it', etc...

Students should use a word processing program when revising. This will make the entire process much easier because students can move paragraphs, delete sentence, and add in words or ideas.

Sentences

So what's so hard about writing a sentence?

That's what I thought before I began teaching. It seems as if the most basic skills, like writing sentences, are sometimes the most complicated. There is more to writing a sentence than meets the eye. Sure, we all know the basics of a sentence, a capital and punctuation at the end, but there are many ways to use sentences.

You can help your child learn about the characteristics of sentences in order to improve your child's writing.

Proper 'sentence' structure first!
Make sure your child always starts a sentence with a capital letter and ends the sentence with the proper punctuation (i.e. question mark, period, exclamation mark).

Have your child become aware of the various types of sentences.
There are several types of sentences:

A) Declarative sentences (also called statements) always end with a period.

B) Questions usually start with one of the 5 W's (who, what, when, where, why) and end with a question mark (?).

C) Exclamations are used to show strong feelings. They always have an exclamation mark (!) at the end.

D) Commands (also called imperative sentences) make a request or tell you what to do. They usually end in a period.

E) Descriptive sentences contain detailed information about something. They usually involve sensory details.

113

F) <u>Run-on</u> sentences occur when two independent clauses are written together.

Flow!

It is important for sentences to flow together. Having good 'linking' or transition words make sentences more fluent when reading.

Variety.

Your child should have a variety of sentence types (as above) in his or her writing. Sentences should also vary in length in order to make readability more interesting.

Having more understanding of sentences will help you to improve your child's writing. Make sure your child edits his/her sentences separately when editing writing assignments.

Types of Paragraphs

All paragraphs have (or should have) a topic sentence that introduces the main idea. The body of the paragraph provides supporting details for the main idea. Finally, a good paragraph should have a closing sentence (unless the paragraph is a narrative which doesn't necessarily give factual information).

There are 4 types of paragraphs:

1. A **descriptive** paragraph describes something.
2. A **narrative** paragraph tells a story.
3. A **persuasive** paragraph discusses an opinion.
4. An **expository** or **explanatory** paragraph explains something.

Descriptive Paragraphs

A descriptive paragraph describes a person, place, thing, or idea. When writing a descriptive paragraph, students should remember to use words that describe the 5 senses (seeing, hearing, tasting, touching, and smelling). Students should remember to tell the reader about the colors, sizes, smells, tastes, and shape things are. It is the writer's objective to make the reader visualize what is being read.

Narrative Paragraph

In a narrative paragraph, students tell a story by sharing and describing experiences. Narrative paragraphs (hence narrative stories) should keep the reader involved and engaged by making the reader want to continue reading. When writing a narrative paragraph, students should include colorful adjectives and descriptive verbs.

Persuasive Paragraph

A persuasive paragraph involves the writer expressing his or her opinion on a topic. The writer wants to convince the reader that his or her point of view is correct and right. Persuasive paragraphs

115

should contain facts and data which support the writer's position. The writer should support his or her point of view the best that he or she can in order to persuade or convince the reader.

Expository/Explanatory Paragraph
The reason for an expository or explanatory paragraph is to give information about a subject. These paragraphs should explain ideas, give directions, or show a process of how to accomplish something. Expository or explanatory paragraphs should have factual information provided in sequential order. The use of transition words is important when writing an exposition.

Although these paragraphs differ in some ways, they still share some common elements. They should all have a sentence that shows the main idea and other sentences that support the main idea.

Types of Writing and Choosing an Audience

In school, students are asked to create specific types of writing assignments.

Writers use different forms of writing such as: poems, friendly letters, procedures, narratives, reports, book reviews, and recounts to name a few. Writers can also combine these forms of writing. For example, a student can write a report that is meant to inform and persuade the reader.

The forms of writing have their own purposes. For example, students can write stories, narratives, plays, and poems to entertain their audience. Persuasion writing involves letters to the editor, business letters, and informative articles with a good argument. Explanations consist of how something works and informative articles are written as reports, news articles, and book reviews.

Knowing these forms helps your child focus the content of his/her writing. For example, if your child is asked to write about recycling, is his/her writing going to focus on the informative aspect of recycling (i.e. statistics about garbage, etc...) and/or is the writing going to focus on the persuasive aspect (i.e. reasons why we should recycle)? Understanding these forms of writing give the writer clear focus and direction when writing.

The audience is also a key factor with regards to deciding on which form of writing your child should use. A good writer should think about the reasons why he/she is writing. The audience (which is usually the teacher), has expectations when reading a piece of written work.

Here are some questions your child should think about before planning his/her writing:

1. What is my audience really looking for? Your child must decide if the writing is going to be entertaining, informative, explanatory, or persuasive.

2. What will my audience want to read in order to keep them reading on? Does your child's persuasive article have strong opinions backed up by evidence and detail? Is his/her explanation organized?

3. Will the audience understand? Make sure your child's writing is not too simple or too complex for the intended audience.

4. Is my writing voice appropriate? If the writing is intended to entertain, it should have a playful tone. Or perhaps the writing is persuasive. Then it should contain a confident voice.

Before starting to write, your child should make a plan. Together, you can decide on the format, the voice, the details, and other characteristics that create a focus and goal that is intended for the audience.

Why Should My Child Have Good Writing Ideas

Students often find it difficult to develop writing ideas. Unless students are given a specific topic with specific sub-topics, students can spend a great deal of time deciding what to write about.

Ideas are the key component of the message insofar as the content of text. The main idea and details hold together the general theme of the piece of writing. Writing ideas should be expressed clearly. Powerful ideas in writing help the reader understand the main idea and theme. The ideas should have specific details and they should be informative so that the reader can comprehend the message.

Regardless of whether your child is writing a personal narrative, a report, or procedure, good ideas will make his/her assignment stand out above the rest.

You can help your child develop writing ideas by using the following checklist:

1. **The writing should be clear and orderly**. The main idea or theme should be introduced by getting the reader's attention. For example, if your child is writing about Ancient Egypt, he/she should focus on an aspect of the culture in the first paragraph, and support the focus in the body of the writing. A good topic sentence and opening paragraph will help your child grab the reader's attention.

2. **Information should be unique and interesting**. Make sure your child's ideas are not simply regurgitated facts. The more interesting the information is, the more interesting the piece of writing will be. For example, assume your child is writing about sharks. Instead of listing the different types of sharks and their sizes, your child can include information about the largest shark ever

119

caught, the uniqueness of the Whale shark, or the evolution of sharks.

3. **Your child should determine important information from his/her research so that he/she seems knowledgeable and informed about the topic.**
   For example, assume your child is doing a report on the Middle Ages. Your child would be better off to include information about the social structure (i.e. the Feudal System) as opposed to the daily life of a peasant farmer. By reporting on the social structure, your child is showing the teacher that he/she understands the key elements of medieval culture. The farmers' roles in medieval culture were significant in their own right, but a report on their daily experiences doesn't illustrate the importance of the culture.

I tell my students that they should try to 'sell' me their writing assignments. They should make them interesting enough that I would *want* to read them.

Vocabulary – Improve Your Child's Vocabulary (Part 1)

A strong vocabulary is paramount for the development of reading and writing skills. The more a student is exposed to words, the better the chances he or she will have in becoming a better reader and writer.

There are several ways that you can help your child improve his or her vocabulary.

Read and Read Some More!

Get your child to read a variety of different texts. Different genres and types of text offer your child a wider variety of words. For example, a book about science, an historical fiction story, a magazine article, and a graphic novel each contain specific words for their respective genre and format. That is, your child will be exposed to science vocabulary when reading a book about space. He will learn new words about society, politics, and culture when reading an historical book, and perhaps some slang while reading a graphic novel.

Show Your Child How to Use Context Clues.

When your child is reading and he/she comes across an unfamiliar word, your child can use a strategy to find out the meaning of the word without resorting to a dictionary (although using a dictionary is ideal, it's not always practical because it may ruin the flow and enjoyment of reading). Have your child try to use another word in place of the unfamiliar word. If your child's new word makes sense as a replacement, then he/she can infer what the unfamiliar word means. Your child can also get an idea about the unfamiliar word by determining whether or not the word is a noun, verb, adjective, etc...

Vocabulary Journal

This is a great resource for students who have difficulty remembering new words. Have your child write new words (i.e. words that he or she has just learned) in a notebook. Have your child periodically look at the notebook. Even if your child doesn't look at the notebook to review his or her words, the act of writing the words down improves his/her vocabulary. Writing down a new word helps your child with future spelling and word recognition.

Get a Thesaurus

A thesaurus will help your child find other words that mean the same thing. This is a great tool for developing a wider vocabulary and learning spelling. I have often had students who purchase a pocket-sized thesaurus (I'm referring to the ones that are actually small enough to fit in a pocket!) and use it in class.

Good Old Fashioned Dictionary

Although tedious, a dictionary is still the best tool for finding new words. Your child's spelling will improve dramatically when he or she learns how to use a dictionary properly. Students will learn the correct spelling, capitalization, syllabic division, pronunciation, synonyms and antonyms, and obviously the meaning of words when using a dictionary.

Online dictionaries and dictionaries found in word processing programs are also easy and fun for students to use and, they help your child improve spelling and vocabulary skills.

Try to get your child to use one or several of these vocabulary-building techniques and you will see a dramatic improvement in your child's vocabulary skills.

Vocabulary – Improve Your Child's Vocabulary (Part 2)

Another way to help your child to improve his or her vocabulary is to learn the structure of words.

Students can figure out the meanings of new words by learning about word parts such as: *prefixes*, *suffixes*, and *root words*.

Prefixes

Prefixes are word parts that come *before* the root word (pre = before). What is really important to know about prefixes is that they <u>often change the meaning of a word</u>.

For example, to know that the prefix 're' means 'again or back', can help a student figure out the meaning of the word 'rewrite' (which means to write again).

Some common prefixes students should know are:

ex = out
anti = against
bi = two
co = with
poly = many
pre = before
re = back or again
un = not

Suffixes

Suffixes come at the end of a word. Sometimes a suffix will indicate the word's part of speech. For example, the suffix 'ly' lets us know that the word is an adverb.

Some common suffixes students should know are:

ed = past tense
er = one who
est = most
less = without
ing = action or process
s = plural
tion = state of

Root Words

Students should know root words because often, when using context clues, students can gather the meaning of the word just by recognizing the root.

For example, the root word 'geo' means earth. So, students can infer that the word 'geography' means the study of the earth, or that the word 'geometry' means the measuring of the earth.

Some common root words are:

bio = life
chron = time
dict = say
equi = equal
fin = end
medi = middle
multi = many

Students should be familiar with common prefixes, suffixes, and root words for their grade level. By having a better understanding of the structure of words, students will become better at decoding words and their vocabulary will improve a great deal.

The Writing Process

Your child comes home with a writing assignment and you're not sure where to start. Sometimes students are given graphic organizers in order to help them with their writing assignments and other times they are on their own. Regardless of the type of writing assignment, your child should approach his/her work in an organized fashion. Some students are able to whip up a report or procedure with their eyes closed but for the rest of the class, well, they need guidance. The 'Writing Process' is a systematic way that increases a student's chances on becoming a good writer. This process incorporates every aspect of planning, writing, organizing, and editing a piece of writing. It's very much like the sculptor who starts off with a mental picture, uses his chisel to shape his work, and finally does the last bit of fine detail.

You can help your child become a better writer by using the 'Writing Process'.
1. **Prewriting** – Decide on a topic and organize ideas. Figure out the purpose for the writing (i.e. who is the intended audience?) and choose the correct format.
2. **Drafting** – Write a rough draft (or rough copy). Create a good 'hook' to get the reader's attention and focus on ideas rather than the mechanics of writing (that will be later on).
3. **Revising** – Share the writing with friends or family members in order to get feedback and make changes.
4. **Editing** – Like the sculptor who smoothes out the fine lines, your child must proofread his work very carefully. He can use a checklist and/or have others proofread.
5. **Publishing** - Publish the writing using the appropriate form (e.g. word processor, fonts, graphics, titles, etc…).

Have your child follow the 'Writing Process' every time he/she has a writing assignment. By following each stage of the process, your child will ensure that he/she becomes a better writer. It all comes down to, practice, organization, details, and effort.

Word Choice

The choice of words your child uses is critical for optimal writing. Having a strong vocabulary is essential for your child to convey meaning. The variety of words that are used in a piece of writing create a rich and colorful form of communication that involves the reader. Good word choice clarifies, illustrates, and expands ideas. The focus of good word choice skills is not to impress the reader (or teacher) with a strong vocabulary; rather, it provides the writer with a more rounded use of everyday words. Students should focus on using proper words in the correct context. After your child writes his/her rough draft of a piece of writing, review the following tips in order to improve his/her choice of words.

- The words are <u>specific</u> and used in the correct context (e.g. instead of , "He walked down the road," we can write, "He <u>casually sauntered</u> down the road,")
- Words should 'strike' the reader's eyes and remain in their minds.
- The sentences should be natural and appropriate for the reader (i.e. is the writing intended for an adult, teen…? Is the reader a teacher or someone else?)
- Use lively verbs (e.g. instead of 'ran away' we could write 'darted off') to add energy to the text.
- Incorporate colorful adjectives in order to paint a better picture.
- Use a thesaurus or a word processor 'synonym' tool.
- Don't try too hard. Difficult words and an over abundance of colorful adjectives can easily tire out a reader.

You can use these strategies to help your child to create an engaging piece of writing that clearly conveys a message in an interesting and natural way.

Writing Basics

Before embarking on a journey with the written word, there are four writing concepts that you must be aware of.

1. **Finding a Topic** – Unless your teacher has given you a specific topic, you should write about anything that interests you! When you write about a topic that interests you, you will be more involved and motivated to do a better job. Finding information and creating the text will be more appealing because if the topic is of interest to you, it will be more engaging. For example, assume your teacher said you had to do a report on Ancient Greek culture and history doesn't interest you. But… you enjoy watching the Olympics on television. Perfect! You can do a report on the history of the Olympics. The key here is to _find_ a topic of interest.

2. **Find Your Information and a Focus** – If you are writing a personal narrative, you just need your own brain because in order to write a personal narrative, you only need your past experiences. If, on the other hand, you are writing a report, you must find reliable sources. Once you have found the sources, decide on your focus. It's easy to get lost in the huge amount of information that's out there. For example, let's say you were writing a science report on the human body. You certainly wouldn't want to write about the entire human body (after all, it takes medical students years to read all that stuff!), instead, focus on one specific aspect of the human body, for example, the eye. The key here is to find a specific topic _within_ a topic (granted your teacher allows you to do so).

3. **Make an Outline and Write Your First Draft** – It's really important to create a graphic organizer (i.e. a chart) to plan your writing assignment. Organize the topic sentences, the paragraphs, and the conclusion. Once you have your

writing organized, you can start on your first draft. When writing the first draft, don't bother worrying about spelling or grammar. It's more important to organize your ideas and make sure that your information is relevant and in proper order.

4. **Editing** - When your first draft is done, you should start editing. Use the spellchecker in your word processor and a good old fashioned dictionary. Use an online thesaurus to make your words more descriptive and lively. Obtain an editing checklist to go over grammar and punctuation mistakes. Make sure you read your writing out loud to catch your own errors. Finally, have other people read over your work and help you edit it.

Follow these 4 writing basics in order to become a successful writer.

BONUS MATERIAL
Part 3
Lessons You Can Do at Home

This section contains some of the lessons you can find at my website Tutorgiant.com. You can have your child try the following lessons right in this book, copy the lessons onto another piece of paper, or create your own lesson.

I have added a coupon at the front of this book for 50% off any membership to my website Tutorgiant.com. There, you will find hundreds of video lessons with worksheets that cover almost every writing skill your child will learn in school. I take up the worksheets in the video to check for understanding.

In the following pages, I have given you several lessons from my website so that you can help your child become a better writer at home.

Primary (Grades 1-3) Writing Lessons

<u>Primary English: Writing</u>   <u>Lesson: Conjunctions</u>

Sentences can be combined when their ideas are the same.
Sentences can be joined with **conjunctions**.
The words '**and**' and '**but**' are conjunctions.

Examples:
David ate his soup + David ate his cookie. =
<u>David ate his soup **and** his cookie.</u>

David ate his soup + David <u>did not</u> eat his cookie. =
David ate his soup but not his cookie.

Combine the following sentences using the conjunction 'and' or 'but'.

1. Shawn played with Robert. Shawn played with Alex.

_____

2. Jennifer likes carrots. Jennifer does not like celery.

_____

3. The bike is new. The skateboard is new.

_____

4. Celine likes fiction. Celine does not like non-fiction.

_____

5. Mark plays basketball. Mark doesn't play hockey.

_____

Primary English: Writing Lesson: Descriptive Writing - Sentences

When writing a **descriptive sentence**, you must create a clear picture of a thing or a person. It is important to write what you <u>see, smell, taste, hear, and touch.</u> This lets the reader understand and picture what you are writing about.

Look at the picture of a park and see how the chart is filled in.

What I can see.	–kids playing -a tree -grass -slide -kids sliding
What I can hear.	–laughing -birds chirping - the wind
What I can smell.	–fresh air
What I can taste.	- nothing
What I can touch.	–cold metal slide - soft grass -slippery slide

Now we can write sentences from our senses. Try to combine the dot jot notes into sentences.

1. I see kids laughing as they go down the slide.
2. The boy feels the cold metal slide as he climbs up to the top.
3. I can smell the fresh air and hear the wind.
4. I can hear birds chirping in the nearby tree.

NOW. Find a picture from a magazine and have your child practice completing a chart like the one above and practice writing descriptive sentences.

131

The purpose of **writing a procedure** is to give clear, simple to follow directions in the order in which they are to be followed.

In a procedure, you must have the following:
1. Write your title.
2. What do you need? (ingredients, utensils)
3. Write down every step in order.
4. Special instructions that are not included in the steps.

Example: Write a procedure for making a pepperoni pizza.

How to Make a Pepperoni Pizza

In order to make a pepperoni pizza, **you need**: dough, cheese, tomato sauce, and pepperoni. You will also need a rolling pin, cheese grater, spoon, oven, and an adult to help with cutting, grating, and cooking.

Step 1: Use the rolling pin to flatten the dough until you get a large thin circle.
Step 2: Take a spoon and spread the tomato sauce all over the dough.
Step 3: Grate the cheese and cut the pepperoni into thin slices.
Step 4: Spread the grated cheese and pepperoni slices over the tomato sauce. Make sure you spread out the cheese and pepperoni.
Step 5: Put the pizza in the oven until the crust gets brown.

Make sure you have an adult help with cutting, grating, and cooking. Never use a knife or oven without adult supervision.
When the pizza is done, cut it into slices and enjoy!

Write a procedure to make a ham and cheese sandwich with mayonnaise.

How To _____

In order to make a

_____

_____

_____

Step 1:

_____

Step 2:

_____

Step 3:

_____

Step 4:

_____

Step 5:

_____

Make sure that

_____

_____

_____

_____

When

_____

133

Primary English: Writing   Lesson: Introduction to Paragraphs

A paragraph is a group of sentences about the same topic.

A good paragraph has the following:
1. The first line is indented (move 5 spaces before typing).
2. The first sentence is the topic sentence which has the main idea.
3. Each other sentence supports and tells about the main idea.
Example:
The first line is indented.   The first sentence is
the topic sentence (main idea).

I enjoy the summer break. The summer is fun. Last year, I went to camp for two weeks. I had a great time. This summer, I will play with my friends and go to the park. The park is a lot of fun. During the summer break I also visit my grandparents and we always have a good time.

The other sentences support the main idea that, "I enjoy summer break,"

Read the following paragraph and answer the questions.

Math is my best subject! Last term, I had an A+ in math. It was my highest mark on my report card. I am good at adding and subtracting. I practice my math every night so that I can do well in math class. My teacher is very proud of me because I always put up my hand to answer questions in math class.

1. Put a check mark where the first line is indented.
2. Circle the topic sentence.
3. Underline two sentences that support the main idea.

Primary English: Writing   Lesson: Personal Narrative / Recount

A personal narrative, or recount, is a retelling of your own experiences.

You are the writer and you discuss something that happened to you.

A recount is written in past tense and is always written from first person "I".

Here is an example of a recount.   **Title**

<u>My Day at the Park</u>   **Setting**

 <u>Yesterday</u> my family and I went to the park.

 <u>When</u> we got there, we took out our sports equipment and played. I first played soccer and then catch.

 <u>After</u> playing, I decided to relax under a tree. I was tired so I asked my family to play cards.

 An hour later, we decided to get our picnic lunch ready. My mom took out the basket and blanket.

 <u>During</u> lunch, a cute squirrel came right up to our blanket. I gave the squirrel a piece of bread. The squirrel ran away.

 <u>When</u> I returned home I read my book and watched television. I had a great time at the park.

1. Notice the <u>underlined</u> 'linking' words that show that the events are in order of time.
2. Notice how each event is in its own paragraph.
3. Notice the conclusion, "I had a great time at the park."

Continued on next page…

Put the following parts of a recount in order in the chart on the next page.

After we saw the African animals, I told my mom that I was hungry so she gave me some lunch. I had my favorite, pizza!

I had a great time at the zoo! I can't wait to go again.

A Day at the Zoo

I went to the zoo last weekend with my family.

When we got to the zoo, I asked my parents to go and see the elephants. The elephants are in the African animal exhibit.

Before lunch, I went on a camel ride. It was really bumpy. I almost fell off!

Title
Setting
Event 1
Event 2
Event 3
Conclusion

Junior (Grades 4-6) Writing Lessons

Junior English: Writing   Lesson: Writing an Explanation

An **explanation** is writing that tries to explain how things come to be or the way they are.

Read the following example of an explanation for the digestive system. You can read the following explanation and the following notes to see how your child should format his or her explanation. Explanations can be written about anything from how bicycles, watches, or planes work. They can also explain how natural events work such as lightning, volcanoes, and tornadoes.

How the Digestive System Works

The digestive system is made up of the digestive tract which is a series of organs joined in a long, twisting tube that help the body break down and absorb food.

The digestive system consists of the mouth, esophagus, stomach, small and large intestine, gall bladder, liver, and pancreas.

First, the saliva chemically breaks down the food and the teeth grind it up so that it can pass down the esophagus. The esophagus is about 10 inches (25 cm) long and it moves food from the back of your throat to your stomach. The J- shaped stomach then breaks down the food into a liquid mixture, and then dumps it into the small intestine. After the stomach empties the food and juice mixture into the small intestine, the juices of two other digestive organs mix with the food. One of these organs, the pancreas, produces a juice that contains many enzymes that break down the carbohydrate, fat, and protein in food. The small intestine is about 2 inches (5 cm) around and 22 feet (7 m) long. It breaks down the food even more so that the body can absorb vitamins, minerals, proteins, fats, and carbohydrates. The liver and gallbladder help the intestine to digest and absorb the food.   Food can spend up to 4 hours in your intestine.

The digestive system is a very important system of the body. Without it, we couldn't get the nutrients we need to grow properly and stay healthy.

<u>Elements of an Organized and Well Written Explanation</u>
1. The 1st paragraph stated what the explanation was about.
2. The second paragraph described the parts involved.
3. The 3rd paragraph (the body) explained 'how it worked' and the 'cause and effect'.
4. The last paragraph concluded the explanation and explained its importance.

<u>Junior English: Writing</u>   <u>Lesson: How to Write a Procedure</u>

The purpose of **writing a procedure** is to give clear, simple to follow directions in the order in which they are to be followed.
In a procedure, you must have the following:
1. **Goal or Aim** – What is to be done?
2. **Requirements** – tools, instruments, parts
3. **Steps** –What is to be done? First step to last step.
4. **Evaluation** – Was the goal or aim achieved?
E.g. Write a procedure for replacing batteries in a remote control car.

Replacing Batteries in a Remote Control Car

If your remote control car doesn't work it probably means that the batteries are worn out and must be replaced in the car and/or the remote.

In order to do this installation, you need a screwdriver with various heads and three AA batteries.

The following procedure will illustrate the correct installation of new batteries.
Follow these steps:
1. Undo the screws under the bottom of the car.
2. Take off the back cover.
3. Remove the old batteries and replace them with new ones. Pay attention to the positioning of the batteries (e.g. + and -).
4. Replace the cover and tighten the screws.
5. Turn the switch on and try the car.
6. If the car doesn't work, repeat steps 1-5 with the remote.

If your car didn't work after switching the batteries in the car itself, then it should work after you switched the batteries in the remote.

Here is a template for you to use in order to write a procedure.

Topic
Goal or Aim – What is to be done?
Requirements – tools, instruments, parts
Steps –What is to be done? First step to last step.
Evaluation – Was the goal or aim achieved?

The purpose of a **report** is to systematically organize factual information to classify and describe something. A **report** involves research to explore a topic.

A report has the following characteristics:
1. A title.
2. An opening sentence introducing the topic.
3. A body that usually contains at least 3 paragraphs. Each paragraph represents an idea.
4. A concluding statement.

How do I start?
1. Choose a topic that interests you. A specific topic is better than a general one (if you have a choice that is). For example, 'Fish' is too general and covers too many areas, but "The Puffer Fish" is specific enough for a report.

2. I will write 4 points I would like to learn and write about Puffer Fish.
    A) Appearance: What do they look like, how big are they?
    B) Special Features?
    C) Behavior: What do they do? Puff up? Food?
    D) What is a Puffer Fish?

3. Now I will organize my 4 points in logical order.
    A) What is a Puffer Fish?
    B) Appearance
    C) Behavior
    D) Special Features?

4. Now I will find information on the Internet, in books and magazines.

5. I will organize my information according to my 3 points. I can simply list my information or put it in a graphic organizer.

Point 1 – What is a Puffer Fish?
-also called the blowfish or globefish
-lives in tropical and subtropical waters
-over 120 different species of puffer fish
-related to porcupine fish
-second most poisonous vertebrate in the world

Point 2 – Appearance
-from 1 inch dwarf puffer to 3 feet long giant puffer
-can puff up because they have elastic skin and no ribs
-teeth sharp enough to cut off a human finger
-upper and lower jaws are fused together
-some puffer fish have spines on their skin

Point 3 – Behavior
-inflates itself with water or air
-blend in with coral and live at bottom of ocean
-can turn themselves into a ball several times their size
-puffers are of few fish that can blink their eyes
-aggressive and guard territory
-can crack open shellfish with their beaks

Point 4 – Special Features
- 1 puffer fish has enough poison to kill 30 people
-they are a delicacy in Japan

6. I will write a topic sentence for each point.
  A) Puffer fish are extremely poisonous fish that have unique abilities.
  B) Puffer fish have some amazing features that allow them to survive.
  C) Puffer fish can easily use their bodies to protect themselves.
  D) Puffer fish have great defenses but they can still be eaten.

7. I will write an interesting introductory sentence. A question or a statement that makes people think is a good way to begin.

8. I will write a paragraph for each point.

9. I will write a closing paragraph that sums up my report.

10. I will edit my work

You can make a graphic organizer like this one to organize your report. Take your point form notes and write them in the boxes.

Title	*Puffer Fish*

Introductory Sentence and introductory paragraph
Have you ever seen an animal blow itself up with air and water?
Puffer fish are extremely poisonous fish that have unique abilities. Puffer fish are also known as blowfish or globefish and are related to the porcupine fish. There are over 120 different species of puffer fish. Puffer fish live in tropical and subtropical waters. They are the second most poisonous vertebrate in the world.

Point 1
Puffer fish have amazing features that allow them to survive. They can puff up in size because they have elastic skin and no ribs. Puffer fish range from the 1 inch dwarf puffer fish to the 3 foot giant puffer fish. The jaws of the puffer fish are fused together and their teeth are sharp enough to cut off a person's finger. Some puffers even have spines on their skin.

Point 2

Puffer fish can easily use their bodies to protect themselves. They can inflate themselves into a ball several times their size by filling their bodies with air and water. Puffer fish can hide on the ocean floor because their colors help them blend in with the coral. They can be aggressive and guard their territory. Puffer fish use their sharp beaks to crack open shellfish.

Point 3

Puffer fish have great defenses but can still be eaten. One puffer fish has enough poison to kill 30 people. Even though they are deadly to humans, some people in Japan eat them. People who eat puffer fish can still die from the poison if the puffer fish isn't cut properly.

Concluding sentence

Puffer fish are one of the most deadly animals on the planet. They bodies and behaviors have allowed them to adapt and survive.

Go to the next page to see the final report.

Puffer Fish

Have you ever seen an animal blow itself up with air and water?

Puffer fish are extremely poisonous fish that have unique abilities. Puffer fish are also known as blowfish or globefish and are related to the porcupine fish. There are over 120 different species of puffer fish. Puffer fish live in tropical and subtropical waters. They are the second most poisonous vertebrate in the world.

Puffer fish have amazing features that allow them to survive. They can puff up in size because they have elastic skin and no ribs. Puffer fish range from the 1 inch dwarf puffer fish to the 3 foot giant puffer fish. The jaws of the puffer fish are fused together and their teeth are sharp enough to cut off a person's finger. Some puffers even have spines on their skin.

Puffer fish can easily use their bodies to protect themselves. They can inflate themselves into a ball several times their size by filling their bodies with air and water. Puffer fish can hide on the ocean floor because their colors help them blend in with the coral. They can be aggressive and guard their territory. Puffer fish use their sharp beaks to crack open shellfish.

Puffer fish have great defenses but can still be eaten. One puffer fish has enough poison to kill 30 people. Even though they are deadly to humans, some people in Japan eat them. People who eat puffer fish can still die from the poison if the puffer fish isn't cut properly.

Puffer fish are one of the most deadly animals on the planet. They bodies and behaviors have allowed them to adapt and survive.

Simple and Effective Ways to Improve Your Child's Writing

<u>Junior/Intermediate English: Writing</u>   <u>Lesson: How to Write a</u>
<u>Descriptive Essay</u>

A **descriptive essay** is a piece of writing that includes specific language, sensory details, and detail.
A descriptive essay is organized like a paragraph. It has a **beginning, middle,** and a **conclusion.**

Steps Required to Write an Organized Descriptive Essay:

1. The <u>beginning or introductory paragraph</u> tells who or what your essay is about. Your topic sentence should 'grab' the reader's attention
   (See the lesson on topic sentences). Introduce 3 major ideas about your topic. A good topic sentence grabs the reader's attention with a surprising statement or a question.

2. The <u>next 3 paragraphs</u> describe and provide detail about the topic introduced in the first paragraph (See the lesson on paragraph writing). Each paragraph should have a topic sentence. Make sure that your 3 topics are interesting. Do your research before you decide on your 3 topics so that you will be able to find the information you are looking for.

3. The <u>final paragraph concludes or sums up the topic.</u> Make sure you have a strong ending.

Take a look at the following chart on the next page. The next time your child is required to write a descriptive essay, refer to the format of the chart so that you can help your child.

Let's assume you are writing a descriptive essay about your favorite superhero. This is what your outline should look like.

Title	Superman
Topic Sentence and Introductory Paragraph	Do you know anyone who wears the letter 's' on his chest? Did you know that the man of steel is the most recognized superhero in the world? (After the topic sentence, I will write my 3 topics)
1st Paragraph Topic Sentence	(This paragraph will discuss how, when, and where the idea of Superman was created) Superman was officially born in 1932.
2nd Paragraph Topic Sentence	(This paragraph will discuss Superman's character, powers, and abilities) Superman stands for truth and justice and he possesses extraordinary powers.
3rd Paragraph Topic Sentence	(This paragraph will discuss the impact that Superman has on culture) Superman's character has led to the creation of many other superheroes and has contributed to the merchandising of numerous products, movies, and cartoons.
Conclusion	(A strong sentence should sum up the 3 topics) Superman has had an enormous impact on children of all ages throughout the world.

Conclusion

In the first section, I gave you 26 practical and effective writing ideas that you can have your child do at home. After reading the next two sections, it is clear that the writing ideas in the first section coincide with your child's curriculum. It is realistic for you to work on a few ideas from part one every month. Don't overdo it. Try to make your child's at home writing meaningful by having it relate to the writing skills your child is learning at school at that time.

The second section will help you, the parent, to understand *how* to help your child. I suggest that you re-read the concepts prior to helping your child at home with each specific skill.

I threw in the third/bonus section of the book because these skills are some of the most problematic for students to learn.

I know that this book will help you help your child improve his or her writing.

Persistence and consistency are the keys to success.

Made in the USA
San Bernardino, CA
21 June 2013